I JUST CAN'T READ MY OWN MIND

Overcoming the Adversities of Life after Stroke: A Play-by-Play

By Bill Hrncir

To: Pam

Focus on your goals, not on your obstacles!

Bill Hrncir

I Just Can't Read My Own Mind
Overcoming the Adversities of Life after
Stroke: A Play-by-Play

Written by Bill Hrncir

Edits by the entire Hrncir Family,
around our dining room table

Cover design by Billy Hrncir

[O] ijustcantreadmyownmind

*I dedicate this book to
my friend and soulmate,
Deedee Hrncir*

*for standing by my side through it all and
helping raise our two awesome kids*

*&
my friend in Heaven,
Arturo "Turi" Alexander*

*for all of the times you came to just hang out
with me after the stroke, bringing me my
favorite snacks, walking alongside me while I
rode my recumbent bike, and filming my son's
games when I couldn't attend.*

Contents

Foreword
By Leslie Meehan

I'll never forget the day I met him. I was working as a speech-language pathologist (SLP) in the outpatient therapy department at Laredo Medical Center in Laredo, Texas. That March morning in 2007, I got my schedule of patients for the day from the secretaries in the front office. I saw his name. *Hrncir? How in the world do you pronounce that?* When his appointment time came, I went into the waiting room and saw a man seated next to his wife (Deedee). She told me how to pronounce their last name "hern-sir." Bill walked with a cane back to the therapy room. All he could really say to me that day was, "Okay." Not his name, or much else. His expressive aphasia (loss of the ability to speak) caused by brain damage (stroke) was quite severe, but his kindness, bravery, and determination were clear to me from our very first meeting. Bill, with the help of Deedee, expressed to me that it had been recommended that he use an augmentative and alternative communication device (AAC) to help him communicate, using which he could select a picture icon or type words that the device would speak for him. When I asked Bill if that's what he wanted to do, he let me know that he wanted to use his own voice. He wanted to get his words back, and that's what he did!

We worked together for a year and a half, and Bill made great progress with his communication—although never as fast as he would have liked. One day during therapy, we were working on phrase completion activities to help him find his words quickly. These activities progress from more predictable, and therefore easier, phrase completions like "salt and . . . (pepper)," "black and . . . (white)," etc. to more open-ended phrase completions like "Why don't you . . .?" "Can I . . .?" There are no wrong answers, as long as it makes sense. I gave Bill the starter phrase, **"I just can't . . ."** motioning for him to fill in the blank, and he quickly responded by saying, **"read my own mind."**

I got chills! I asked him if that's what it feels like to have aphasia, and he said, "Sometimes." Now, when speaking about aphasia to others, he explains that "my brain holds my words hostage." What a vivid image that is, and a helpful way for those of us who have never experienced aphasia first-hand to get a glimpse of what it must feel like. I knew that needed to be the title of a book to help support stroke survivors and caregivers in their journeys through recovery. That was over thirteen years ago.

Our families have remained close friends through the years, and we have followed Bill's recovery journey closely. Bill and Deedee are an inspiration to so many people in a multitude of ways. Bill is a no-holds-barred kind of guy. Tell him he can't do something, and he'll prove you wrong. Never walk again? Wrong! Never run again? Wrong! Never ride a bike again? Wrong! Never run his businesses again? Wrong! You'll read in this book about his hard-working, driven, aim-for-excellence personality, all of which have served him well in his recovery. Any therapy technique, diet or lifestyle change, exercise, or book he heard about to help stroke survivors, he tried it, changed it, worked at it, read it! There was nothing too hard and nothing he wouldn't try to help himself improve. And not so he could get back to the way he was pre-stroke, but so he could be his best self now, in the present, and continue getting better.

He has truly embraced his stroke and the recovery process as part of his story, with incredible grace, and has used it to help others. Bill has inspired so many other stroke survivors in their recoveries, helping them to believe in themselves, despite the odds stacked against them.

Deedee, his wife and steadfast ally, is an exceptional example of love, faithfulness, and commitment. In addition to supporting Bill through his journey, she helped found the Laredo Stroke Support Group, and gave hope and community to so many who desperately needed it. Their children, Alli and Billy, and their families, have been constant sources of joy and strength as well.

Bill mentions the importance of laughter in his book. He loves to laugh! I'll never forget how much we laughed together during our therapy sessions. He would say something he didn't mean to say, like calling the TV "pudding" (that's aphasia for you!), and he would just start laughing, which would make me laugh. He had the most contagious laugh but, as he laughed, he would point to his mouth and motion with his hand like, "I have no idea why my laugh sounds like that." He told me even his laugh changed with his stroke. His laugh is wonderful, and it's that ability to find joy in the face of seemingly insurmountable obstacles, along with his incredible determination and hard work, that have gotten him this far on his stroke recovery road and will carry him the rest of the way.

I am thankful to know Bill Hrncir and honored to have been part of his journey. It's safe to say I learned as much from him as he did from me. He has an inspiring story, so I'll let him tell it . . .

Introduction

The year this book was published, I turned sixty-one. My stroke was fourteen years before that. Pre-stroke I wanted to write a book about coaching strategies in the game of basketball. After

Fly, Billy, fly

Junior College Basketball Game, doing what I loved most

growing up around the sport, playing from first grade on and later coaching my son, it was one of my strongest passions when my stroke hit me. Over the years, I had researched skills and fundamentals through sports, all in the hopes of writing a guidebook. Then my stroke came along, and it changed my plans.

Lucky for me, coaching basketball and recovery after stroke go hand in hand. Both take perseverance, dedication, a positive mindset, and grit. So, as you read through these pages, whether you are a stroke survivor, a caregiver, or just someone who wants to read about overcoming obstacles, you're in for a

One of our many basketball huddles with my son and his friends during a game

pep talk. Get comfortable, huddle up, and in the words of my brother-in-law, Craig, (in response to his kids when they say "life's not fair,") welcome to "Real Life 101."

When my stroke hit me, my life was

Coaching my son, Billy, during a T-ball game

sports. In my thirties and forties, I was both an athlete and a volunteer coach. I coached my son from kindergarten through high school in football, basketball, baseball, and cross-country, all along continuing to compete in running and cycling myself while working out to keep my body fit.

Working with a stroke survivor buddy as he practices balancing on the bike.

After the stroke, my volunteer coaching spirit thrived. My wife and I established a local stroke support group in our community, and it was only natural that I took some of the other survivors under my wing. I helped encourage them to stay healthy, stay active, and stay positive.

I'd be lying if I said the road to recovery wasn't a little rocky. In my experience, the two main vices for survivors are either the inability to muster energy to feel good again or the stubbornness to create a new normal. They are so determined to do things the way they used to, that they don't work on the therapies and rehab that could help them. Personally, I had to come to terms with the fact that recovery would take much longer than I expected, but to stay positive, I surrounded myself with other survivors and a support system of people that would keep the momentum going.

When I first started writing this book, I thought I would just speak to other survivors who needed that same spirit, but as I sat down to write my memories, I realized that everyone around us play into the recovery process. It's not just about the survivors. It's about their families, their friends, their caregivers, and the medical professionals that surround them for the years following their stroke. The role of the caregiver is so pivotal, and at times they are not sure how to handle their role in this stroke adventure. When real life feels unfair, the most important thing is for us to unify and accept the help of those around us, instead of hiding away from the world. Stroke can be tough and it can make you feel helpless, but so can any big life change. The only way we get through it is together.

I hope this book motivates and helps you on your road to recovery, whether from stroke or from other obstacles that have knocked you down. My story of resilience will show you that life is a marathon, not a sprint. You've got to take it day by day, and you have to be patient and honor where you're at in the process.

Similar to a playbook, these pages will point you in the right direction, because after all, we all do better with a little bit of coaching along the way. You don't have to use my methods, but you can definitely learn from my journey.

If I can overcome my stroke, you can overcome the trials in your life, too!

Chapter 1: The Perfect Storm

I was a super dad, loving husband, businessman, and an athlete. At that time, I was forty-seven and healthy, or so I thought. Then, out of nowhere, I had a severe, knock-me-down, take-away-my-voice, and throw-me-into-a-wheelchair *stroke*!

My stroke reminded me of *The Perfect Storm*, written by Sebastian Junger about the 1991 storm that hit a fishing boat, the Andrea Gail. They are confronted by three raging

weather fronts that unexpectedly collide to produce the greatest, fiercest storm in modern history. My stroke was the perfect storm, plus one: genetics, overtraining

The Andrea Gail, internet search image

in my running (of all things), the stress of running my businesses, and witnessing a traumatic death. The raging fronts met at the wrong time!

Wrong End of Genetics

My brother, Eddie, is the oldest, and I am five years younger. In the middle are my two sisters: Mary Ellen and Nancy. Eddie and I

The Hrncir Hurricanes (our family track relay team name): Eddie, Mary Ellen, Nancy, and I

were always trying to one-up one another. For example, when he was living in Austin, I called one day, wanting to gloat, "I flew the ultralight with precision take-off and landing." (It's a small airplane that weighs less than three hundred pounds. You can legally fly it without a pilot's license.) Eddie responded,

Me, flying the ultralight

"I took off in the ultralight with pontoons on the lake, flew around for a while, and landed on the lake." In that instance, I guess he had one-upped me!

The Hrncir blood is genetically geared for stroke. My dad left this earth by stroke when he was eighty-

My father, Leon, my brother, Eddie, and I, a few months after my stroke

six years old. My mom is about to turn ninety and has suffered a series of mini strokes.

15

Eddie had a stroke, and one-and-a-half years later, I had mine. I had an ischemic stroke followed by a hemorrhagic stroke that resulted in the loss of sight in my left eye. I had one-upped Eddie this time.

Overtraining

Since the age of six, running was in my soul. I still remember my first cross-country tryout at a local baseball field. From that day forward, I competed in school athletics that involved running. From the time I was twenty-five until my stroke at age forty-seven, I ran all kinds of races; 10Ks, 5Ks, 1-milers, 800 and 400 meters. I was obsessed. I ran in hundred-plus-degree weather, through injuries, and took no days off.

Obsession, however, can backfire, and I overdid it in my forties. Fifty-six-year-old sports cardiologist and runner Dr. James O'Keefe says, "Exercise is probably one of the single best things you can do for your health, but if you overdose, you start getting other effects that outweigh those benefits, and in extreme doses they

Reaching the finish line back in the 90s

even have fatal complications."

The bottom line is that when you get to forty, you have to be more moderate about your exercise. "Run for your life! At a comfortable pace, and not too far," said O'Keefe at a TED x UMKC presentation. Like any potent drug, exercise too little and you are not going to gain. Exercise too much, and it will cause injury. I now try to aim for smarter and more restorative types of exercise that boost longevity and agility in my joints, like biking and yoga.

Work-stress Overload

Whether you run a small local business (like I do) or run a multi-billion-dollar corporation, stress is inevitable, but we must learn to manage it. The American Institute of Stress says job-related stress is broken down like this: 46 percent is workload, 28 percent is people issues, 20 percent is the demand of juggling personal and professional life, and 6 percent is lack of job security. I agree with their classifications of stress, but for me, people issues and juggling personal and professional life are the toughest. I am inherently an entrepreneur in everything I do, so I naturally tend to take on more projects than I should at once, and I set the bar high for my achievements along the way. My wife has lovingly referred to me as a workaholic, and there were times I owned four businesses at one time (all in completely different fields).

Present day, I own two businesses, even knowing that they're not the best for my overall health, but at least I downsized a little. I can honestly say that I thrive on these adrenaline rushes, but no one can live like that for long periods of time. Only recently have I come to terms with the mantras "Keep it simple" and "Take time out," and to be honest again, only because of the neurological fatigue that comes with life after stroke am I forced to slow down and take breaks. Otherwise, I might have never stopped living that way.

Surviving a Trauma

Our hometown, Laredo, is hot for ten

months of the year. This day, though, was cold and rainy. On that dreary day in November, the year of my stroke, I got a call from the office: "Checks are ready, Mr. Hrncir."

The intersection where the accident occurred

On my way there, right in front of my warehouse, I stopped by the oncoming traffic with two lanes zipping beside me. As I waited to turn left, a car came towards me! The driver was swerving, and just in the nick of time, the car ricocheted off the median barrier and flew over my Tahoe. It was an unbelievable nightmare before my eyes!

I unbuckled my seatbelt, opened my car door, and looked behind me. I saw that the car had landed directly on the car behind me, and the driver of the car on top hightailed out of sight. As I frantically scanned the scene, I saw that a little boy in the passenger seat of the crushed vehicle had blood all over his body, and I could hear him crying, "Papi! Papi! Papi!" I quickly pulled the boy out of the car. Buried under the tire was the boy's dad. There was no way that he was still alive.

What seemed like an eternity later, but was actually just fifteen minutes, a fire truck arrived on the scene. I stayed with the boy in my arms until the EMS paramedic took over, and all I could think was, *There is blood everywhere*. My clothes were covered in his

A visual of my dreary memory

blood. Dazed, I walked down the hill to my steel store. I could not shake what I had just witnessed.

I called my house from the office, and my daughter, Alli, answered it. I said, "I witnessed a wreck by Laredo Discount Metals and I'm coming home. I don't want you to freak out, because I am covered in blood, but it's not mine. I'll explain the details later, but I'm calling to ask you to boil water for a hot drink and turn on the shower. I'm wet and freezing and I can't stop shaking. I'll be home soon."

When my wife Deedee came home from school, my jacket was on the washing machine and it was still full of blood. I had the fireplace turned on and a blanket covering me, but I still could not stop shaking. Deedee immediately asked what had happened, and I told her the story.

Though my body was physically cold, there was no doubt the chills were coming from the fact that I couldn't shake the memory of what I had just seen: how somehow my life had been spared, and the life of another was taken right in front of my eyes. That night, at two or three in the morning, cold sweat poured from my body. People react to traumatic events in different ways. I felt numb in the beginning, and then for several nights, I had flashbacks of the little boy crying and of the car flying over me.

I know I was in shock, not just that day, but for the two weeks after that leading right up to my stroke. Some of my close friends were skeptical that the emotional trauma of what I saw could have caused my stroke. I have read several articles, including one by Steve Kim, MD, in Healthline, that state that experiencing a traumatic event can cause physical, emotional, or psychological harm. I know in my heart that the accident was a huge contributor.

I'm on a multi-year odyssey, but I still have a little more to go. If you're holding this book now, chances are you've either survived a stroke, know someone who has, or want to prevent one. Even though we all have different risk factors for stroke, I hope you can take away the most important reminders: manage your stress, exercise with awareness, and take time to slow down and smell the roses.

Enjoying a special moment with my granddaughter at a Laredo Stroke Support Group Event

Chapter 2: The Day that Changed My Life

A few days after the accident, Deedee and I invited my friend Arturo to eat at Danny's Restaurant. I was suffering from a really severe headache, which Deedee thought was strange, because she was the one who typically experienced them. Little did we know that such a rare headache was a very important sign of what would completely change our lives.

Still shaken up from the accident two weeks prior, I offered to drive Alli to Seguin right outside of San Antonio for a special event where she was performing. Since Deedee was feeling sick, she stayed home while I drove both Alli and her friend. I would have six or seven hours of fiddling around, so I thought I might as well run on Lady Bird Lake in Austin.

I was enjoying a run around the lake, but fifteen minutes into it, I totally blacked out. I imagine I hit the ground like a rock. After five minutes or so, I woke up, but it was foggy—I was foggy! I saw a runner stop near me and heard him calling 911. I slipped into a deep sleep.

The policeman who arrived took my key fob from my pocket (since that is all that I had on me) and went back to where the cars were parked. The officer clicked and clicked until he

The brick that my family dedicated at the spot on the lake trail where it happened

identified my car. There, in my car door, he found my wallet and cell phone and called Deedee. "Your husband had an accident. Call Brackenridge Hospital and they will explain." Deedee pleaded with the officer, "You can't tell me anything? Can you tell me if he is okay?" She expected the worst.

She called the hospital and the nurse said, "We think your husband had a stroke. Do you have the power of attorney to speak for him? His best chance for survival is a clot removal procedure." Lost, confused, scared, and heartbroken all at once, Deedee didn't know what to do next.

Meanwhile, my son Billy was at the movies with his cousin Kenny. Billy's phone vibrated, and as he said hello, he heard Deedee crying and explaining that I had suffered an accident. They sprinted out of the theater and headed home, coincidently, on the same highway where I had witnessed the accident.

Deedee called her sister Bucca and her husband Bill T., who lived down the street. Bucca answered the phone and Bill T., to this day, says that the look on her face summed it up. She told him that I had collapsed while running and that they should rush over.

Once Bill T. got to the house, Deedee told him that I was in the hospital in Austin but that things weren't clear yet. He called his buddy Richie, who lives in Austin and is a mutual friend of ours. "I was supposed to run with him!" Richie said. He hurried to Brackenridge Hospital to get an update for them.

Once Billy got home, Bill T. saw his scared face and said to him while placing his hands on his shoulders, "Who has been in the best shape of their life?" "My dad," Billy answered. "Yes, your dad has been in top shape, whether it be physical or mental. Say some prayers." He calmed everyone and insisted on driving them to Austin. He pushed a hundred miles per hour.

In the car, Billy frantically called his coach and said that he was not going to be at basketball practice. Through his tears, Billy was calling everyone he knew to tell them that we needed prayers and we needed them fast!

In the meantime, Deedee called my sisters and the school where she was teaching, to tell them the news and to say that she would be out and to pray. All the while, they still had not been able to get hold of Alli. Her ringer was off since she was about to go on stage. Finally, Dara, our niece, went to find Alli in Seguin. An hour into the drive, Richie called Bill T. and confirmed, "He had a stroke."

My buddies, Richie & Vic, visiting me at Texas Neuro Rehab, about a month after my stroke

Chapter 3: Faith, Hope, and Perseverance

Faith

I was raised Catholic, and I believe in God. I truly believe that I could flash back to any given point in my life, and no matter how tough things got, there was always a constant: my faith.

Reflecting on the moments leading up to my stroke, I'm in awe at how the events played out. For many years, I would wake up before sunrise to go running, as early as 5:30 a.m., with a flashlight mounted on my head. The dirt road I would take ran just below the Tex-Mex railroad tracks and wasn't exactly the safest area to be alone in the wee hours of the morning. Along with the rattlesnakes, it was dangerously secluded, but something about the beautiful sunrise helped me pace my run before I'd head back home to start my day. So, what made the morning of December 9, 2006, any different?

First, instead of my usual run, I dropped Alli, my daughter, off at the dance performance in Seguin, and headed to Austin.

Second, instead of my usual secluded run in Laredo, I chose a popular trail in Austin where the runner found me and called 911. He was an angel in jogging shorts. What could have been a moment of disaster and chaos, turned out to be a miracle.

Third—and here's the real kicker—my supposedly random choice of Lady Bird Lake in Austin happened to be located only a few short miles from Brackenridge Hospital, one of the largest stroke health systems in the United States. Any stroke specialist will tell

An old picture of Brackenridge Hospital, which no longer stands.

you that "time is brain," (which refers to the brain cells that are lost with every second that passes without treatment for a stroke).

There's no other explanation that I can think of except that my faith brought all of these "coincidences" together on that day. It almost seems they were pivotal stepping stones that I did not know I was taking.

Dr. Camp, the neurologist, heard the stroke alert down the halls of Brackenridge Hospital. My stopwatch (which was still running) had me there in thirty-eight minutes from the beginning of my run. The CT scan revealed that I had an ischemic stroke, which results from a clot, on the left side of my brain.

I was given an injection of tissue plasminogen activator (tPA), a clot-busting drug. One in three patients who receive tPA resolve or have major improvement in their stroke symptoms. However, according to the American Academy of Neurology, in six out of hundred patients, bleeding can occur in the brain and cause further injury like serious long-term disability or death. In my case, the leak caused my brain to swell, and nothing was working to stop it. Time was of the essence!

Eventually, the doctors decided that our only hope was to try a craniotomy, where a section of the skull, called a bone flap, is

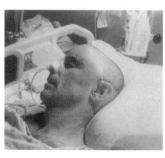

removed to allow the brain to swell after the stroke. The bone flap is frozen and replaced several months after recovery. I guess I should add here that I was forced to wear a goofy helmet that I was not okay with, and my

A few days after my stroke. Notice the staples and my sunken in head, where they removed a piece of my skull to help with swelling of my brain.

supportive friends went through the trouble of getting a legit bike helmet so that I would wear it and follow the doctor's orders. It was the little things like this that mattered most to me. Having friends and family around to make me feel like an athlete, remember my strength, and to help me feel loved was a blessing that I won't ever take for granted.

I would have never thought that professionals in the medical field would have such a tremendous impact on my life after stroke. The individuals that have crossed my journey since 2006 have really come out of the woodwork and have truly gone beyond their role of doctor, nurse, or therapist. My neurologist, Dr. Sanchez, became a bike riding companion, my nurses became encouragers, my therapists became defenders, and all became friends.

In a stroke survivor's critical time of stay in the hospital, immediate assistance, advice, and, most

The rehab center in Austin, Texas where I started my recovery journey

importantly, answers are sought out from surgeons, doctors, or nurses. In between the doctors' consults, frequent nurse check-ins, therapy sessions, and family visits, there are other individuals that patients encounter on a more regular basis: those that drop off food or clean the patient's room. These people are

often overlooked and usually slip in without notice. It is not expected that they have the answers a patient is seeking. In fact, it's rare that a conversation goes beyond a "Good morning" or a "Thank you." Yet, it is people like Vern, a staff member whose main job was to transport

Vern, one of the first angels I met at TNR

patients from one room to another, who made me feel important during this vulnerable time in my life. Vern was one of the first people I interacted with at Texas Neuro Rehab Center in Austin, Texas. "Ready to go?" he asked as I very quietly sat in my wheelchair. Unable to speak because of my aphasia, I glanced and nodded at the strong, tall man at the door entry. The amount of strength he had was doubled in his courtesy. His kindness was the hope I needed to believe recovery was possible. Then there was Cindy, an

occupational therapist at the rehab center, who, even though she wasn't assigned to me, would stop at my room three or four times a week to

Cindy & I, at TNR

exercise my affected arm. While she was there, I could also expect to say some prayers together and be reminded of my faith when I needed it the most. Both Vern and Cindy were my angels.

Right after my stroke, I did not feel afraid or even nervous. In fact, I clearly remember thinking that my recovery may take a couple of months—after all, my brother recovered at a fairly quick rate. I hadn't noticed at all that my speech and movements were incomplete, and my body wasn't responding to my desires. In my head, I could hear myself thinking, even though it was a little messy in there. I had no idea the number of setbacks I'd have to overcome.

I will say again that every stroke is different, and every recovery process is different. I quickly learned that mine was not like my brother's, and my stroke was not similar to a swollen ankle or a sprained muscle that could heal in a few weeks. My personal knock-me-down, take-my-voice-away, throw-me-into-a-wheelchair stroke meant it would take decades to recover. Upon our arrival home, after being in Austin for months, it was tough for our entire family to know what to do next. My wife sought resources in our local community, but there was no stroke support group to answer the question, "What next?" The hospital suggested she start a group herself, but how could she possibly think of starting a group to be there for others when we couldn't show up for ourselves yet? Again, we wouldn't let that hold us back, and Deedee started by reading every stroke book she could find cover to cover over three years, and eventually we had enough knowledge and resources gathered to share with others. It took several tries to get it right. We started hosting meetings at a hospital, but the clinical feel and the restrictions that hospitals have to follow didn't set the tone we were looking for. Something was missing.

Once we identified that faith was the answer, we contacted Monsignor Alex, our parish priest, and asked him to start announcing our meetings after each Sunday mass. Thus, the Laredo Stroke Support Group was born. Each month, we invited specialists to talk about resources available, and after getting feedback from the survivors and their families, our offerings eventually expanded to healthy snacks, exercise ideas, goal-setting, and more.

How we have grown! 2019 Laredo Stroke Support Group Christmas Party at San Martin de Porres Church

We were invited to an art show hosted by the Border Region Behavioral Health Center, where we learned more about how art can be used as therapy

Left to right: Omar Salinas, survivor, Bill Hrncir: survivor, Paty Orduna: Art Heals Director, Samuel Piton: survivor, Ruben Gutierrez, survivor

for those with mental health issues such as depression. We met an amazing individual named Paty Orduna, whose passion for healing goes beyond her artistic abilities (she is a great painter), and touches the lives of so many Laredoans. Paty told me, "We can never heal alone. People who are lonely and do not feel loved will never heal." That's why her program is called "Art Heals." She says that having moments of darkness or

Paty and I at an Art Heals class

vulnerability is important, because through that darkness, you search for light. The art classes we now offer for stroke survivors are not really about the art we produce, but more about the overall experience. Paty says the healing begins the moment the survivor chooses to wake up in the morning, get ready for class, and show up. Then it continues when we socialize as equals, offer constructive criticism to our peers, and fix our mistakes. When we present the final project, we feel pride and experience ownership. And the healing finally comes full circle when we sell our art to someone else and they become part of our healing process. That brings us together. I strongly feel that this is another stepping stone that God has given me. Bringing Paty into our group was no accident.

Antonio Gonzalez, Ruby Olivares, and Dan Ridge at an Art Heals class

My hope and perseverance are rooted in faith. Monsignor Alex says that we like to set goals and plans for our lives. With something like a stroke though, we're forced to change our lives radically, and we have to adjust. We like to be in control, and when something threatens that, it is a great challenge that often causes us to question our faith. When we don't have the answers that satisfy us, it leaves us feeling empty, and we wonder why we can't get our health back.

Sometimes religious leaders or friends will ask us to pray or trust in God. If we don't have hope, our thoughts can go to "What's the use in praying if God is not there? I feel like God has abandoned me." In my personal experience, having a strong sense of hope has let me keep those negative moments away and my faith strong.

Hope

After my stroke, everyone in my life thought I'd never walk or talk again. Even when the social workers told my wife to install a wheelchair shower and ramps at our house, I knew in my heart those would be out in a few months and I'd be walking again. The hope I had in my heart spread to my family, and it kept us all thinking positively. I understand that not all survivors can muster up hope from within.

Monsignor Alex said, "Our words can have an impact on stroke survivors, but our actions speak louder than words." As stroke survivors, the best thing you can do for yourself, and to inspire other survivors, is to get out there.

• Go to therapies and group classes.

• Send other stroke survivors reminders about meetings.

• Offer them a ride if they won't go on their own.

Armando, Ruben, and Hector, my stroke buddies, practicing balance on the bike

Be persistent, and help them find the perseverance, because after all, things require more effort now. Just a simple trip to the store or an appointment can take an extra hour or two to get dressed and get in the car, which can be discouraging. Having an accountability buddy helps more than you know.

Some survivors may not feel like they have someone cheering them on or believing in them. In fact, some survivors live alone, and divorce rates tend to increase post stroke. That's why it's so important to reach out to each other . . . to be patient with each other. Not only are you a beacon of hope for others, but for yourself.

Personally, I never had space in my heart or mind for fear, only hope and faith. It's like a muscle you have to flex, and with years of practice, love, and support all around me, I've trained the muscle well. Even when things wouldn't go my way, there was always a lesson to be learned, and I always felt stronger because of what I'd been through.

Perseverance

My college basketball teammate Walter said, "Championships are great, but when the odds are against you and you overcome people's expectations, that's something that I draw back in my life's adversities and challenges and realize that things aren't always predetermined. And if we really battle through that, adversity does build character." My relationship with Walter provided camaraderie. We encouraged and supported each other's strengths. We challenged each other to improve our weaknesses.

It was 1978 when Laredo Junior College (LJC) was matched up against Houston powerhouse San Jacinto Junior College (San Jac). In this particular game I warmed the bench, but my upperclassmen taught me how to overcome obstacles on this unforgettable night.

San Jac was ranked nationally, and it was a "refueling stop" where Division I potential professional athletes would stop and play for two years to bring up their grades to major college standards. Players ranged in height from 6'4" to 6'10". By comparison, we didn't have anyone over 6'4" in height, as LJC was on the border of Texas and Mexico. Naturally, LJC didn't place any players in the NBA. All season long, we were up against towering teams throughout the nine-member Texas Junior College Athletic Conference.

Just like my stroke buddies now, my teammate Rusty had the mindset that taught us to have each other's backs. My other teammate Bruce explained it like this: a team of small players can equalize a talented tall team with good fundamentals. Even though we were smaller, we had trained hard. Mechanics, technique, and muscle memory were one part of the equation. The other part was confidence in our shooting. On top of that, where the other team lacked heart and character, we had endurance—being persistent and playing hard the entire start of the game so the other team got tired and we could finish strong.

I remember Coach Segler saying, "We do not have any one outstanding player.

We've got to depend on the team concept." If you look at the individual stats of our players, they were pretty awesome, but what impressed me the most was all of the assists and teamwork that got us the win. Coach Segler trusted our players' instincts and instilled confidence in us.

Of all the players in that game, David stood out to me the most. I admired the way he confronted the challenge, and even I was intimidated at his confidence. He persevered, regardless of how the odds were stacked and regardless of what the outcome of the game should have been. With a minute left, he stole the ball! It sealed our victory. The final score of the game was LJC 100 to San Jac 97, and it was the biggest win in the history of LJC. David had true grit, and our guys had perseverance.

In the huddle with Coach Siegler. That's me in the back center, hanging on every word.

LJC shocks San Jac

By JOHNNY CAMPOS
Times Sports Writer

The way San Jacinto head coach Ronnie Arrow chased referee Fred Thill off the court after the Texas Junior College Athletic Conference game between his Ravens and Laredo Junior College Friday night in Maravillo gym, it didn't take a genius to guess who had lost the game.

The Palominos registered their most prestigeous victory ever, 100-97, in downing the Ravens, a name synonymous with the TJCAC championship.

LJC hosts Lee at Maravillo gym tonight after evening their conference record at 2-2 and upping their season mark to 7-8.

The Ravens got off on the wrong foot in the contest, with Roderick Austin drawing a technical for wearing a choker. Rusty Segler, who tallied 16 points in the affair, was successful on the free throw after sinking the game's first basket to give the Herd a 3-0 lead.

Hugo Chaparro, who matched Segler's total, added a basket for LJC before the Ravens could generate any offense. But San Jac used their superior height to take easy short jumpers from inside the key.

Larry Spriggs was the main culprit for the Ravens, sinking five first-half buckets, but the Golden Herd kept pace until 11:55 to go in the first half.

With the score tied at 25, Terry Henderson went on a tear, netting five quick points to give the visitors a 30-25 advantage.

San Jacinto upped its lead to 40-33 with 5:58 to go in the first period before baskets by Gogi Kramer and David Robeau pulled the Palominos within three.

But the Ravens took the momentum just before the half, highlighted by a slam dunk by Spriggs past Segler with 2:31 on the clock for a 48-41 lead.

San Jacinto went into the dressing room with a 54-45 advantage, having hit on 20 of 44 first-half attempts and 14 of 18 shots from the charity stripe.

LJC hit an even 50 percent in the first half, netting 21 of 42 shots, but in the second half is when the Herd found their range. Bruce Carrier in particular.

Carrier, the game's high scorer with 30 markers, tried to bring the Palominos back single handedly, netting three quick fielders in the opening minute of the second half.

Segler added a basket to pull LJC within three at 58-55 with 17:30 left on the clock.

The Ravens then scored eight of the next 12 points to widen their margin to 66-59, but the Herd kept fighting back until finally, with 11:32 to go in the contest, Carrier, who hit on nine of 12 second-half shots and netted all four free throw attempts, put the Palominos in front at 73-72.

San Jacinto evened the score at 73 with a free shot by Terry Henderson, who contributed 22 to the Raven total,

but LJC kept hitting from all spots on the court, upping their lead at one point to 85-79.

In the second half the Palominos hit for a sizzling 76 percent, connecting on 23 of 31 shots, many of them set up by the playmaking of Kramer.

Kramer handed out 15 assists, Segler eight and Chaparro seven, and the Herd kept breaking through the Raven press to score on easy layups.

Arrow kept commanding his troops to, "Deny! Deny!"

The Ravens did deny LJC somewhat with their press, tying the score at 89, but Kramer, Chaparro and Segler began to break the press to set up some three-on-two situations for easy scores in the closing minutes.

Roderick Austin netted two of his 12 points with 1:34 on the game clock to knot the score at 95.

Kramer then hit one of two free shots and David Sanchez tallied on a layup for a 98-95 advantage.

On the ensuing play, Sanchez stole the ball down court, and the Palominos had the ball out of bounds with 30 seconds left on the clock after one of 27 Raven turnovers.

Segler missed the first end of a one-and-one situation, but Kramer tossed a crisp pass to Chaparro under the San Jacinto basket following another Raven turnover to seal the win.

David Robeau netted 14 points for the Herd and hauled down six rebounds. San Jac won the rebound battle 43-26.

Curtis Phauls hit for 24 for the Ravens and Mike Potts added 11.

Perseverance in the Court, not on the Court

Thirty-one years later (almost three years after my stroke), I was not standing on the basketball court, but rather in the courthouse. I had received a letter saying, "You are hereby commanded to appear and answer before the Honorable District Court, 49th Judicial District, Webb County, Texas, at the Courthouse of said county in Laredo, Texas, at or before 10 o'clock on the 20th day of July, 2009."

Since successfully running my father's storage business, and taking it over more than twenty years before, things had never led in the direction of a letter like that. The Mexican peso devaluation in August of 2008 made that year for my company, LMS International, a tough one. Even though the peso had recovered about half of its lost value, my Mexican customers and I were broke.

With my father, Leon, representing our Moving & Storage company.

Before we go any further, let me give you the full picture. Back in my early twenties, Laredo Moving & Storage was in trouble financially and didn't have much hope for growth. With a lot of elbow grease and my business degree, I was able to turn things around with a team of hard-working individuals beside me. My entrepreneurial spirit led me to go beyond just getting the business out of the red, and we developed into LMS International, an import/export and warehousing distribution center. On top of that, I also co-owned two other businesses: Laredo Discount Metals and G&H Logistics. LMS was a three-warehouse operation and we grew to surpass all of my expectations, but you better believe that the stress that comes from running a business like that undoubtedly contributed to my stroke.

Nine months since I was physically out of the office post stroke, my brain wasn't ready to get right back into things and my body was still tired. Even when I returned, aphasia made it difficult for me to communicate. To just jump back in where I left off was almost impossible, and as I mentioned, I only had half of my brain to work with now.

Even though I had a solid team of managers and personnel, every team needs a coach to guide the plays along the way. Two of my businesses remained steady during my absence, but one in particular got behind very fast. Paying off the principal loan of our three warehouses, combined with county taxes, district taxes, and payment plan for the four cranes, and the multiple forklifts and railcar mover was

The LMS International Warehouse

overwhelming. When times were hard, we fell behind very quickly, and soon we owed a little over $3.2 million. I took the letter of summons to my accountant, and we began the process of filing for re-organized bankruptcy. I still cringe when I think about it. Though my mind wasn't at 100 percent, my heart felt the defeat as deep as you can imagine. Regardless of the dire circumstances, I knew we had to find a solution. As American author Josh Shipp once said, "You either get better, or you get bitter." I decided that we would get better!

When moments in life, like my encounter with bankruptcy, challenge me, I have those basketball memories to guide me. Aside from the sports influences in my life, I also had business partners with a lot of experience and knowledge to share, and they reminded me of my perseverance. The debt had accumulated to the point where the only way to pay it off was to sell one of the properties. With the sale of that warehouse, a portion was paid off. As for the outstanding taxes and rest of the warehouse loan, they graciously worked with us to set up payment plans, which we strictly followed until we cleared our name. I endured four nail-biting years, but I got through it and I paid it all back.

Dr. Zelena Montminy says that, without the momentum that comes from perseverance, we can't bounce back from the challenges that knock us down. Otherwise, we would never get back up. Perseverance is what gives you the ability to quickly adapt when things don't go your way. If you don't have that, you'll never reach your goals in recovery, or in life in general.

Stroke survivors, I know it may seem bleak, but trust in the influential people around you. I had my teammates, my business partners, my spiritual leaders, my family, and my friends from Laredo Stroke Support Group. Help is out there for you, but you've got to get off the couch!

Chapter 4: Laughter is Good!

About eight years ago, as I was driving back home and headed down the street to my house, out of the corner of my working eye, I saw a man walking with a cane. I quickly noticed the two most obvious physical effects of a stroke:

· walking with a limp: check

· raised and tightened arm on one side: check

Could he be a stroke survivor? Might he need someone to connect with? I circled the block, but he wasn't there. Something told me to keep looking for him. I drove a few blocks further, and saw him go into a dollar store. Like a kid ready to meet my future best friend, I parked and got out. So full of excitement, my aphasia completely kicked in and I lost all words. I walked up to him and tried to get the words out. He immediately could tell that I was a stroke survivor, too. We bonded. I invited him to our next stroke support group meeting, and the rest is history.

Sammy's laugh & smile are contagious

Samuel (Sammy) Piton is, in my book, the "stroke survivor

of the century!" In his twenties—twenty-eight to be precise—he played on a darts team with a local club. One fateful day of their tournament, Sammy took one aim, threw the dart, and he had a stroke! He couldn't speak for ten years, and his arm and leg were paralyzed throughout. As his friend, I can say that Sammy has more than made up for the

Even when Sammy's shoe came off during a ride, he couldn't help but laugh.

talking, because he will now carry on a conversation with anyone for as long as he can. We love Sammy. His unique way of beginning the sentence with English and ending in Spanish (or vice versa) and his gregarious personality make him so fun to be around. Did I mention he is now fifty-three, and he giggles through life?

It is very hard for stroke survivors in general (myself included) to deal with the depression and disability caused by a stroke. I think laughter does well to ease our situation for even just a minute. When I meet other survivors that feel the same, it brings us closer together and we can relate. We all want to be surrounded by positivity, and we appreciate the distraction. Sammy is always down for a good laugh, and that feels good.

I love laughter! The angels I've encountered on my stroke journey all have their unique way of spreading humor to those around them. Personally, I really appreciate and admire how my therapists (especially Mary, Amy, and Leslie and her family), other stroke survivors (like Jesse, Dan, and Sammy), and volunteers (like Rick, Javier, and Jesus) spread happiness to those around them through laughter. I get a kick out of it!

Back in 2013, I received therapy through the neuromuscular retraining program with Amy Silver, a senior physical therapist at Saint David's Medical Center in Austin. We used biofeedback and pool exercises, and Amy said that, through repetition and practice, and making that connection stronger, we made small changes in my actual range of motion and strength. She also said that me just getting on a bike or other piece of equipment and her barking orders would not rebuild those connections as much as if my brain did the work itself. It was obvious when we worked together that Amy loved working with stroke survivors. Her humor made the work fun, and I would have been miserable if she had been a biofeedback drill sergeant. I still believe she was put on this earth to spread laughter and fun with me and all the stroke survivors she worked with. I remember laughing and giggling out loud during the session, when I still could not yet talk!

Saint David's Medical Center's biofeedback method is called the Brucker Method, and I was their guinea pig. (Note: The program is internationally recognized as the biofeedback method and was created by Dr. Bernard Brucker at University of Miami's School of Medicine. Check it out if you are a stroke survivor.) In the late 1960s, doctors

originally viewed biofeedback with suspicion, because it wasn't fully neuroscience, nor fully

Working with Amy at St. David's

rehabilitation. It was something new. Basically, they would place electrodes on different muscles, like my bicep (arm) and temporalis (scalp). Each electrode was a different channel, and Amy would ask me to do a certain movement and then we would observe how my brain connected to the correct channel. If it was not correctly responding, we knew what to work on. This was tough work, and it wasn't always fun to hear that my brain was broken. Who else but Amy could make me laugh when I was otherwise not happy with my poor performance? I've already told you how competitive I am, and I can tell you I didn't want to admit that my brain needed rewiring, but Amy's never-ending jokes kept me in the game longer and I didn't want to give up.

Sure, I could have asked any doctor to prescribe an antidepressant, and I'm not sure if laughing a lot actually counts as medicine. But I can tell you that laughter unites and brings people together like no other.
Ask any of the greats:

Philosopher Bertrand Russell said, "Laughter is the most inexpensive and most effective wonder drug."

Audrey Hepburn said, "Laughter cures a multitude of ills. It's probably the most important thing in a person."

Herman Melville said, "I know not all that may be coming, but be it what it will, I'll go to it laughing."

Lee Berk, an associate professor at Loma Linda University in California, said, "Laughter appears to cause all the reciprocal, or opposite, effects of stress."

If you ask me, laughing is as important as exercise, eating right, and getting enough sleep. It is a useful tool to fight the anxiety and depression that come with a stroke. It improves blood flow and memory and decreases inflammation, which is very prevalent in most stroke survivors. If laughter appears to be good medicine, then let's do it! I declare, "A laugh a day keeps the doctor away!"

Laughing with my mom

Chapter 5: Hitting the Reset Button

A year-and-a-half before my stroke, my brother Eddie had a stroke. When it was time for me to begin my recovery journey, I thought to myself, *Eddie came out okay. I will too.* I didn't know I was a much more extreme case with deeper damage. Instantaneously, half of my brain, left eye, and right arm and leg were in shambles.

My brother, Eddie I

My bandaged-up mind remembered how active I used to be, but my cognitive and physical activity were going to take a little time—okay . . . an incredible amount of time. My brain said, "I can't find the words! I can't run! I can't weightlift!" My stroke buddy Hector said, "Stroke is not a death sentence. It's a reset button!" I know that the degree, the severity, and the deficits that follow are different from Eddie's (right hemisphere) or Hector's (left hemisphere) or

Me, Hector, and Sammy after a bike race in 2018

anyone who has had a stroke. I am in it for the long haul, though. My recovery is measured not in years but in decades. It will take a very long period of time, but that's okay. The expectations I have for myself are important because they have me fighting every day to never give up and continue to make progress. It's a day-by-day thing, and a step-by-step process.

In order to think about recovery in steps, I have to look at my areas for improvement one at a time. So, what exactly were my deficits following my stroke? When I was admitted to Brackenridge Hospital, they said I suffered a CVA or cerebrovascular accident on the left side of my brain. I was dubbed the "stopwatch guy" because I had arrived unconscious and without identification, and the EMT said that my stopwatch clocked in at thirty-eight minutes. I was a forty-seven-year-old runner that had the misfortune of a CVA or stroke.

tPA, a clot-busting drug the doctor gave me, is known to cause bleeding and cause further injury in six out of hundred patients; thus, I now have half a brain. But in retrospect, I would do it all over again. Honestly, because it still saved my life—well, that and a craniotomy. They cut out a piece of my skull to relieve the pressure on my brain. This is serious stuff that I am glad I was not aware of until after the fact.

I was drugged up in a nice way, but my family, in particular my wife, sat dazed, wondering if I would ever come out of it. At that point, I could not utter a word, and I don't really know if I even realized how long this was going to affect me. I was responding to simple commands, but not all the time. I was groggy a lot of the time and could not even see clearly. I remember my immobile arm and leg, my lack of speech (aphasia), my feeding tube, so many questions floating through my head, so many wires and tubes attached to my body! At one point, according to my wife, I tried to pull everything out and jump out of bed. They strapped me down so I couldn't go anywhere.

I spent two weeks at Brackenridge, and then it was on to Texas Neuro Rehab Center (TNC), where I was drugged up for the ride over. Upon arrival, I heard the therapist talking to me, but I could not answer. *Duh! You drugged me up*, I thought. For those first two

My son and daughter, beside me at TNR

days, I had a "Popeye" face: one eye closed, unshaven, beanie on my head, and pretty awful-looking. I vaguely remember starting speech therapy within three or four days, which was when I began my recovery odyssey with a somewhat sedated body and a foggy brain full of questions that I could not ask.

At TNC, I met Jean Moore, the first of my speech therapists. She gave me an evaluation to see if I could swallow yet. I flunked, although not miserably, and speech

therapy began, consisting mostly of nods and grunts. I did comprehension exercises where I could show that I understood her questions and

Jean & I at TNR

prompts helped too. She worked with me on swallowing and uttering sounds. Jean showed genuine concern for me, and because it was such an important part of me starting to talk again, we worked together to get my feeding tube taken out.

At one point, she was contemplating whether or not to put me on an AAC, an augmentative and alternative communication device used to speak or write for those with impairment from a stroke or other brain injury. From what Jean knew about me so far, she knew I would want to speak for myself. She cared about me; not just the patient in Room 101, but me. TNC cared about me, too, and this was comforting to know.

Living with Aphasia

I remember I was told to exercise my vocal cords. Not having many other scenarios to compare it to, I remembered back to when Eddie went to speech therapy. After just a couple of weeks, voila, his speech was completely back to normal. I didn't know then that I had aphasia. Anyone who has had aphasia understands how awful it feels when you literally have your voice taken away. On top of that, I had trouble hearing. Instead of being able to tune in to the sounds around me and dial in on what I wanted to hear, it was a jumble of noise and a nasty "auditory overload." Mostly, I miss the conversations that I use to have with my family, my friends, and my customers. Even though I can be physically in front of someone, and I can hear them talking, it takes my brain longer to absorb the information, process it, and come up with a response. When it comes to casual conversations, I'm blessed to have people in my life who have learned to be patient and wait for me to try and get full sentences out.

Otherwise, if they answer for me, I never get a word in. I have to remind myself every day that not everyone understands that it takes patience to have a meaningful conversation now . . . and it took a lot of work to get to where I am at. I got help from a very unique group of experts.

I drove to Austin for about five years, getting up before dawn on Wednesday to drive to Austin Speech Labs, and driving back home (a three-and-a-half-hour drive that took me almost five because of traffic) late Friday night. Why would I make such an effort? As soon as I met Shilpa Shamapant and Shelley Adair, co-founders of ASL, I saw their

Shilpa, myself, Shelley, and Deedee

approach to therapy was unique. As speech therapists themselves, they saw a gap in insurance coverage and the potential a survivor had to get back to being functional. Shilpa says, "Functional is such a relative term. There isn't one standard 'functional' for every survivor." ASL has been in operation for over twelve years, and their philosophy is based on the fact that therapy should be affordable, intensive, and offered for as long as the client needs to reach their full potential. She explains it as though stroke survivors are students learning a language. You wouldn't just practice a new language a few times a week for a short amount of time each day. It takes consistent practice, homework, and conversations to be proficient.

The difference with stroke survivors is that, as adults, we have an inbred dictionary that associates categories and memories in our brain. So, it's not like when a child is learning a sound by association. She used the example, when they first opened, of my good stroke buddy Casey. When he

Deedee & I with Casey and his parents

was learning to talk again, and Shilpa was using sounds (like M, mmm, mom), Casey would respond with his mom's name (M, mom, haaaa, Helen). It taught her that stroke survivors' brains work differently, and that she would have to find a new approach. That's one of the things that kept me coming back— their unique approaches and their dedication to finding innovative ways that are actually effective.

When I think back about the homework I was assigned, I cringe, and then I laugh. It began, usually, on Sundays. My daughter Alli and I would sit down at the kitchen table, and I would do it. I would try to just get one sentence out. Just one. Alli would repeat the sentence, and then I would repeat it, but my brain would take the words and mix them up or throw in a word that was not in the sentence. She would say, "Sorry, Dad, that's not the right word." I would stare at the words and point to the letters, but my brain would interfere. My letters were so jumbled that Alli was really not making sense to me. As frustrating as it was, we couldn't help but laugh at this new lesson on humor. I eventually graduated from sentences to paragraphs.

My wife Deedee, as a kindergarten teacher, would supportively help me work on my reading in bed at night. I would practice reading aloud, and she would watch me struggle, wanting to help correct the sentence. I would throw in words that weren't there, and eliminate words that were. By the time I'd get the sentence right, I would forget what I had just read, with no comprehension of it, and have to read it again. Talk about frustrating when you're trying to read a story and make sense of it. Later on, I learned that highlighting as I go and practicing every day helped immensely so I don't lose my spot and I can remember what I read. I also practice writing and rewriting things I read. For instance, my home office is filled with piles of spiral notebooks where I have rewritten some of my favorite chapters, important paragraphs, and inspirational quotes. It helps me understand them, solidify the ideas in my brain, and then access them later when I'm writing. My wife and my daughter help me clear out the clutter every few weeks, once I've incorporated the ideas in my writing. God help me when my phone eventually crashes, because I also have gigs of memory on my phone taken up by all of the notes I've stored on my calendar, my note app, and countless others.

Austin Speech Labs taught me so much, but especially how important it is for a survivor to be a part of establishing their own goals for therapy and recovery. If someone simply tells you what you need to achieve or accomplish, you aren't as vested as you are if you create the goal for yourself. Shilpa recently reminded me of a time a few years into my therapy when my daughter was getting married. Even though at that time I was focusing on my physical therapy and rehab, she said she saw a shift in my intensity and focus on speech from one day to the next, because I started prepping my speech for my daughter's wedding. It meant a lot to me, as the head of my family, to achieve that milestone, and I had work to do. Once I declared that goal for myself, it became something I could work to achieve.

Once I achieved that milestone, it was on to the next. As a leader and coach in my community, and now as a stroke survivor, I

wanted to be able to help others in similar situations and to spread the word for stroke awareness. So, after I did my time at ASL through group, individual, computer, music, and

Giving my speech at Alli's wedding, with Deedee by my side

brain game therapies, it was time to venture out on my own, with a desire to help others. Shilpa encouraged me to speak in front of

audiences, and so I did. At the age of fifty-three, I became a public speaker. Who would've thought a stroke survivor with aphasia could become a public speaker?

Speaking at Hope Rocks, LSSG Benefit Gala in 2018

From 2013 until 2018, I delivered about seventy speeches with the help of a visual presentation of pictures and videos of my story to civic organizations, colleges, elementary schools, and rehab centers.

I will never forget the tremendous amount of support I received from the University of Saint Augustine in Austin, Texas. They allowed me the opportunity to return at least six times over the course of two years, to speak with their

A group of students at the University of Saint Augustine

occupational and physical therapy students. What stood out to me the most was their patience and their interest in my recovery journey (and that of my stroke buddies' that I took along for the ride). After my speeches, they'd use us as guinea pigs to test out their physical therapy methods. We were very willing participants.

Saint Augustine students practicing therapy methods on me

These speeches helped me work on memory, sentence structure, and overall spontaneous speech. On post-speech Q&A, I would warn people that my speech recovery is still not complete. Spontaneous speech is tough, even now.

Auditory Overload

It's been over a decade since I first began working with Dr. Sanchez, my neurologist. Now that we look back, he reminds me about when I first returned from Austin, and the initial shock of it all; the damage to my brain was so significant. I mostly suffered with conveying ideas. Aphasia was taking over my communication. "In Laredo, you have a pace of life that is still a little slow. You have time to smile. We have to look each other in the eye. If you were living in a high-paced city like New York City, it would be a different story for a stroke survivor. They don't have time to listen. You're out of the game immediately."

Early on, when I'd go to a restaurant, a store, or on a doctor's visit, I would find a way to get their attention without words: using loud gestures and grunts. You can imagine me like a confused caveman. Eventually I was able to communicate a somewhat clear, concise message, but man did it take work. Exhausted, but happy to have been able to get the message across, I tried to always keep a smile, and I think that's what helped people be more patient with me.

Listening and processing are still obstacles I deal with on a daily basis. Remembering back to Halloween 2014, my wife and I went to a superhero "dress up" party hosted by my daughter and Casa Yoga at Border Foundry Restaurant. The meal was served inside the restaurant, but the party was celebrated outside on the patio. It was a crisp and cool fifty degrees outside, and I was cold! When my wife and I got seated, immediately I was hit with so many different sounds, smells, and sights. It was an overload for my senses in an uncomfortable way. Even though I wanted to enjoy

At the party, trying to have fun, but really struggling on the inside.

the night and celebrate with my family, little things like the seemingly quiet buzzing of six or seven mosquitos as they got a little too close to me, or the swinging of the restaurant door open and closed as it flapped the leaves of a plant by the entrance, were just too distracting for me to even listen to what my wife was saying. I remember wanting to connect and network with my daughter and some friends, but between my body temperature and all of the other external forces, I just couldn't focus. It was an awful feeling. All I wanted to do was get into a quiet space.

Jon Caswell wrote an article called "Sound Advice," and said, "Aphasia is a language disorder but it can be a hearing disorder too. It's not that survivors with aphasia can't hear; they have difficulty processing what they hear." Caswell interviewed Mary Purdy, professor of speech-language pathology at Southern Connecticut State University. She stated, "Simplistically, auditory overload is just too much info coming in at once for the brain to process. It doesn't even have to be language; it can just be noise."

Caregivers and loved ones of a stroke survivor, especially when he/she has aphasia, the best thing you can do for them is just be patient. Wait for them to get the words out. It may seem like forever, but their mind is like a very complex filing cabinet. When you try to guess, it just frustrates us even more. Don't be afraid of stroke survivors with aphasia. They may seem different, or like something is wrong, but inside, there is someone (their pre-stroke version) dying to communicate and be an active part of society again. You can help them feel that again, if you stay patient.

Aphasia Recovery Connection says, "Aphasia affects language, not intellect." That's a very important distinction for us all to remember when interacting with stroke survivors.

The Road Back from Spasticity

Another roadblock a stroke survivor may encounter is spasticity. In my case, when I least expect it, my muscles become trapped with stiffness and tightness, and that's a problem for daily functioning. It has always been a goal of mine to regain performance of activities required in daily life, but the problem is that there is no one blueprint for all survivors. Since each of us is uniquely affected, each must find our own path to recovery, and different doctors and therapists have their own views or ideas.

I imagine it something like a peloton of angels cycling to my rescue. My path was a mix of occupational therapy and physical therapy, and continues to be something that I work on every day. Each therapist has blessed me with the knowledge and experience they have in their own field. For instance, Katie Rusnak, my occupational therapist at TNR, worked using neurodevelopment training. We wanted to tackle simple things like holding toothpaste and putting on deodorant, trying to open doors, open the fridge, drawers, etc. She helped me practice those things on a daily

basis. Patrick Reetz, my physical therapist, also from TNR, had me try neuromuscular facilitation techniques on my leg. My favorite thing about Patrick is that he was patient; he knew that learning new skills (or re-learning old ones) takes time and

Katie & I working on mobility in my arm, wrist, and hand at TNR

practice. Since he was a musician, he compared it to learning to play the saxophone

and would say it may take someone four, five, six, or even ten years to master. It takes motivation and support. We worked a lot together on stimulating my

Patrick is an awesome musician and inspired me to stay patient

nervous system to excite the proprioceptors to get the desired movement from my leg.

Jennifer Perez Del Rio, my occupational therapist from St. David's Medical Center, determined that she would try neurodevelopmental treatment (NDT) on my affected side. Jennifer would challenge and force my body to use the affected side, even if it didn't work as well and was harder to use.

That way my brain could build new connections to make up for the parts of the brain that are damaged. That is called plasticity, when the brain can change its own functioning depending on the changes within the body. Using that method over and over again with repetition, she would push me to my weaker side and force me to stand on it. She would secure my strong hand, keeping the left side (my strong side) from overcompensating for my weaker side. NDT included lots of hands-on work like climbing a ladder, pulling a ladder, and pushing a chair. The work we did together helped me find some improvement

Jennifer, and the team at St. David's Medical Center, working on my affected side

on my stroke-affected side, and even though I'm not at 100 percent yet, I experience movement in that hand and leg.

Years later, Jennifer and I joked about the challenges we faced. Number one , I was a leftie. The stroke happened on my right side. That meant that the right side was never used

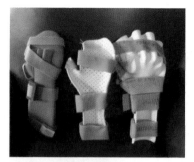

Some of the many hand & leg supports that we tried to support mobility of my affected side

to having to work that hard to begin with. Number two, since I was a competitive athlete at heart, that meant that my strong side automatically would always try to take over. It took me years to admit that, but I finally understand that I have to resist the urge to cheat with my strong side.

One of the things Jennifer would mention often is that, even when a patient might put in the effort in therapy, when they go home, they often return to their comfy spot in their recliner. From that seat, their caretaker looks after them, and they become a crutch. Even though they are trying to help, they enable the survivor, and the therapy stops there. Often, they expect the results to just happen overnight, and when they don't see things get better, they become more and more depressed. In turn, they never get better. She said, "The way I see it, as a therapist, my job is to teach people how they can continue to heal themselves and what they can do to still work on those things, because it's not just what you do in therapy, but it's what you do outside of therapy." I tell all of my stroke survivor friends all of the time, "You *have to* get an accountability buddy," who can be either another stroke survivor you can work out with, a trainer, or a friend or family member who will encourage you positively.

A few weeks into therapy with Jennifer, she recommended I go see a physiatrist who could help us tackle the immense rigidity in my arm and leg. She felt it would help us make steadier progress in our sessions if we could just get that side of my body to cooperate a bit more. Ever the eager student, I marched right up to his office on the second story. The placard read "Physical

Dr. U gave me hope for restoring functionality

Medicine and Neurotoxin Institute." Dr. Joe Urquidez strives to restore functional abilities like walking and running in stroke survivors like me. He explained how important it was to continue working with Jennifer on the root problem, and that Botox would be a temporary treatment to help restore the brain-muscle connection. Botox doesn't solve the spasticity, but it generates the opportunity to exercise. Because the stroke damaged my brain's ability to send signals to my muscles to move, I needed some help to loosen up my muscles temporarily, so that I could exercise them in hopes of rewiring my brain for the long term. To combat that, about three times a year, for two years, Dr. Urquidez would inject little bitty injections in my limbs. Putting mind over matter, I told my brain the injection felt good even though each one was a pretty intense prick. Like Jennifer, he said that, even though it was his job to provide the tools to help me improve, in the end, the outcome would still equal the effort I put in. I couldn't stop doing important therapy exercises. I learned so many over the course of my therapies, and I have shared the most beneficial ones in the next chapter.

When I exercise, ride bikes, or spend time with my stroke buddies, I think about how important it is for all of us to get our weight-bearing exercises in. Even though they can seem tedious compared to fun things like riding a bike or running, these exercises are crucial to work on that brain-muscle communication, and in my particular case, if I don't do them five days a week, come Monday, I'm back at square one.

For me, this was one of the pivotal moments in my recovery where I finally felt the athlete in me resurge. Dr. U's idea of restoring functionality was a beacon of hope for me. Instead of just basic movements, we both established that our end goal was to come full circle and get back to the level where I wanted to be. He understood my ambitions and helped me work towards them.

Not every day of a survivor's therapy is a win. Some days, there are setbacks. But it was nice to leave Dr. U's office and, after a few days, see the results I was looking for. I would celebrate the win for the day.

Recovery can feel like a full-time job, and it can sometimes feel like there is no end in sight. For me, recovery is a five-day, two-and-a-half-hours-a-day program. That's what works for me. The most important thing is to try hard to surround yourself with individuals who will put you in a great mood and help you celebrate the little wins. I keep hope and fight for a possibility or a chance, building up my confidence in anticipation for the results that will come with practice and consistency. I have faith in my doctors, therapists, family, and other stroke survivors.

When my astrologer and magician brother Eddie and I talk about our recovery, he always brings up Isaac Newton. Newton was one of the fantastic minds of the seventeenth-century scientific revolution. Eddie explained Newton's calculus theory of

the "limit" to me. With the "limit," you are getting a half of a half of a half of a half over time. Eddie told me and my stroke friends that stroke survivors' recovery is like the calculus' limit. The progress is steadily getting better, but improvements become progressively smaller over time, to the point where we can

Thanks Eddie, for reminding me that a small victory, still means a victory

barely tell we are, in fact, improving. So, if we don't give up, we will continue to recover, but in much smaller increments. Stroke survivors, stay positive. Avoid negative thoughts that keep you from believing in your little victories along the way. They will pay off over time. Even just now as I type this, I was able to, for instance, spell the word astrologer when in the months after my stroke I would literally stare at a paper for hours not able to even get two letters in a row correctly. I'm here to tell you that it is possible and that *you can do it* because *I did it*.

Monocular Vision

Perhaps one of my least favorite deficits after the stroke was the lack of vision in my left eye. Even though I knew something was definitely off with my vision, it was hard for me to communicate that to anyone. While I was in the rehab hospital, my family made a nice bulletin board with pictures of my parents, siblings, and kids. They added my track accomplishments to motivate me. It wasn't until much later that I explained I could not see it from the bed, but I was grateful for their efforts nonetheless.

To put it simply, our eyes, just like all of our other organs, depend on the flow of oxygen-rich blood to perform properly. When signals to the brain are cut off, that can lead to permanent vision impairment, and eventually blindness. In my case, the doctors said I had a cerebral stroke and an eye stroke simultaneously. According to Stroke.org, up to 66 percent of all stroke survivors will experience some change in their vision following the event. It is estimated that approximately 20 percent of them end up with a permanent visual field deficit.

I remember my field of vision felt immediately different when I woke up at the hospital. It was like looking through a camera lens that was shrunken to a keyhole. On top of that, everything was blurry. By the time I was taken to the rehab center, the scope of my vision had broadened, but things were still blurry. Keep in mind I still couldn't talk at this point, so there was no way for me to communicate this. On my last days there, I received a final diagnosis before heading

Matching eye patches: My friend, Michael Portman wears one because of an accident in college & I was starting therapy at Texas Neuro Rehab Center after my stroke

home. The doctors ruled I had Horner's syndrome in my left eye. They gave me an eye patch to see if that would allow my right eye to focus better, but now we know that vision was already gone on that side and the damage was permanent. This marked the end to visual acuity in my left eye. The clearness and the sharpness of my vision is just a memory.

Not being able to see with my left eye and not being to control my right side created multiple issues with balance, aim, and overall coordinated efforts. Deedee and I joke about how we have to choose if I want to see her with my right eye but barely be able to feel her holding my right hand, or if I want to feel her holding my left hand but not be able to see her in my left eye. For all I know, she could be sticking out her tongue at me and I'd never know.

Very early on, my ego took a hit. Imagine being a busy businessman, used to driving across town daily to check in at various locations, then heading to coach your son after work, and getting in your own daily workouts. I was used to being 100 percent independent, and my loss of vision put an end to that for a short amount of time in my recovery. By the time I appeared for my two-hour-long driving test, it was perfect timing. My brain fog had lifted a bit, and I felt confident to drive again. I was lucky that the DPS who took me on the drive was patient. He tested my vision, and my cognitive ability to remember how to get to places of importance like work and home. He allowed me to drive him all over Laredo. Looking back now, my hunch is that he wanted to be confident with his stamp of approval, knowing that my wife and family wanted to feel safe with me back on the road. If you're a stroke survivor reading this, remember vision isn't the only setback in getting back on the road. Cognition and memory are equally important to keep yourself and others safe.

I know that I am blessed to be able to drive, read, write, use my phone, etc. I don't have to depend on others. Being able to see, even with just one eye, is huge. I have learned little tricks that help me work with my blind side. When I am going to sit in a group, while dining or visiting, I can position myself where I will be sure to see those that I'm with. On my vehicle, I installed an extra pair of mirrors on top of the rear-view mirrors to allow me to see several angles at once.

I think, as much as it hurts me to say, and it hurts me to hear, as stroke survivors, we have to be willing to accept our new normal. While I value the process of getting multiple doctors' opinions, when you have a unanimous recommendation that eye surgery will not bring back your field of vision, spend your energy and resources on adapting to your new normal rather than on surgeries that will not reverse the effects of the stroke. Every survivor is different, and we all have varying degrees of what can be fixed, depending on our timeline. I had to learn to be patient with myself and with others. As Frank B. Brady, author of *A Singular View*, says, "If the surviving eye has poor vision and is also the secondary eye, then it's going to take more time and effort to adjust." Age is also a crucial factor. The younger you are, the easier your body can adapt.

Many of the survivors in our group can't drive, read, or even do easy tasks owing to visual field loss, double or blurry vision, and lack of visual processing. It's hard to even name one other stroke survivor who doesn't have some kind of vision impediment after the stroke. Each year, an estimated fifty thousand Americans enter the world of the one-eyed. For many of us, it happens without advance notice. In *A Singular View*, Brady talks about intelligent adaptation to living with one good eye. Because there are not a lot of resources available for the newly one-eyed during the awkward and sometimes risky period of adaptation, it's important for family members to be as helpful as possible, and look to your local support group or for online resources that can help you find ways to adapt. This is one of those amazing areas where we can be of support and strength to each other, because it's not until you're going through this that you understand how to overcome it or learn to live with it on a daily basis. It took us a few years to find the right resources, but our group now practices techniques for gauging depth and distance in many of our weekly activities.

Balance Phenomenon

Dr. Sarmati of Stroke Therapy (R)evolution asks an important question: "Would we be able to skillfully handle our equilibrium even without looking, if we did not have the exact perception of where our legs and feet are in respect to the rest of the

Mando practicing gliding

Jesse with a pedal-less bike

body?" As a stroke survivor, there was a time when I couldn't feel my affected limbs at all. Whether intense temperature or intense pressure was applied, I was completely oblivious. Now that I have some sensation back in those limbs, re-learning how to balance my body has been a hurdle. I like to think of it as both a mental and physical challenge because a lot of sustaining balance comes from mental focus and concentration, but it also requires knowing how much force to use to physically move my limbs. Even then, I can mentally push with all of my might to raise my affected arm, but that doesn't mean that it will do what I want it to, when I want it to.

This balancing act used to mean I would fall down a lot . . . more than you can imagine.

I know many of my stroke peers do, too. Here's where that perseverance comes in handy. Basic actions like walking are more difficult now, not to mention tougher tasks like riding a bike or jogging. The slightest mental distraction like a bird in a tree nearby or the honk of a car horn can throw off my focus while bike riding, and then my balance is off again. Anxiety creeps in, then panic, and then comes the fall. It happens in the blink of an eye, and before I know it, I'm showing up at home and getting scolded by my wife for a

scrape on my leg from falling. It has gotten better over the last few years. Now falls happen once or twice a year instead of every week or so.

Me & my bike falling, captured thanks to my Go Pro

Ruben Gutierrez: Like a Phoenix, He Rises

Confucius said, "Our greatest glory is not in never falling, but in rising every time we fall." Never have I met a man who embodies that quote more than my stroke buddy Ruben. We met on purpose, when my son-in-law told me

Ruben & his son using the tike to practice balance

79

he saw someone who looked like they had survived a stroke at a rec center in his neighborhood. He was impressed with his dedication, and thought I might like to invite him to our meetings. I walked right up to Ruben, introduced myself, and we walked the track and got to know each other.

The common denominator in our friendship is that Ruben and I both thrive

Ruben, riding with our LSSG Riders at the park

when we have a race to look forward to. It keeps us motivated to work harder in our recovery journey. In Ruben's case, his stroke left behind tremors in his arm and leg that made it very difficult to ride a bike again, let alone get on one. Balance was almost impossible, since he had very little control of

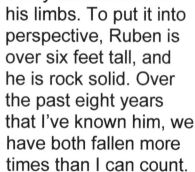
Ruben & his son riding with the LSSG Trike

his limbs. To put it into perspective, Ruben is over six feet tall, and he is rock solid. Over the past eight years that I've known him, we have both fallen more times than I can count.

Some were falls off our bike; others were just walking on uneven ground. Either way, we both manage to get back up. In Ruben's case, after eight years of practice, he can now ride a bike on his own.

Armando Martinez: Brain Dead to Bike Rider

During the first few years after the Laredo Stroke Support Group was formed, Armando and I bonded at one of the meetings, over our love of cycling. Pre-stroke, Armando rode his bike everywhere, including an eighteen-mile route to his parents' house a few times a month, over and back. We both missed competitive biking so much, and it was refreshing to find another survivor that understood what that was like. We would get together two to three times a week to practice, and I was enthused to have a friend to coach.

Therapist, Bob Whitford, assessing Armando's range of motion

Practicing "feeling free"

It was an honor to help another survivor find confidence on the bike like I had achieved. We were up against many obstacles: my aphasia, his depth perception and balance, and our brains against our bodies. When it came to communicating with each other, the frustrations rose quickly. Luckily, we both have a sense of humor, but when I look back, I'm reminded how brutal those moments of training were. Over a span of three years, we worked together, and Armando achieved the goals he set for himself each step of the way. Every day we raised the bar just a little. We began with simple and basic gliding from one cone to another, indoors. We progressed to easy pedaling, and then moved outdoors and practiced tuning out distractions. Eventually, we rode down to the lake and back, riding over hills and small bumps. Then we rode trails at the ranch. One of his most recent achievements was racing forty-two miles from Zapata to Laredo, Texas.

Armando riding from Zapata to Laredo.
Race duration: 42 miles

After a recent bike ride with Dr. Sanchez, we got to talking about Armando; he is both of our neurologist. Dr. Sanchez mentioned that, when Armando got to the hospital, he had suffered a hemorrhage in the brain, and cardiac arrest. They flew him to San Antonio, where the doctors ruled him as "brain dead" and ordered for him to be sent home to spend his final days with family before unplugging him. Dr. Sanchez examined him, and even though he was in a coma, when they would stimulate his larynx, he would let out a weak cough. He knew this to be contradictory to a "brain dead" diagnosis and had hope that, as long as there was some responsiveness—even if that was the only one—there was still a chance for recovery. He ordered another CAT Scan. The scan showed that the hemorrhage had drained into his ventricles. That can be hard to detect, so he figured maybe the San Antonio doctors had missed this.

As the days went by, little glimpses of hope emerged. Day two brought on his gag reflex. They adjusted his treatment to reduce the swelling in his brain. Day four he began to respond to light, open his eyes, and blink. He then started to breathe on his own. Day seven he made eye contact and was able to track with his eyes. If we fast-forward to him riding over forty miles on the bike, how can one not believe in miracles?

Our determination helped inspire each other. It didn't take long before other stroke survivors started to join Armando, Ruben, and me for bike rides. With the help of Laredo Stroke Support Group board members, we were able to secure funding and donations for bikes, trikes, and even a trailer to haul them to the park on Saturdays. After a few years running, we finally have a tight-knit group of volunteers and survivors who are die-hard. Rain or shine, we are there twice a month for biking, laughs, and camaraderie.

My personal journey has implemented many different types of traditional and non-traditional therapies. I think each survivor has to find ways to work on their deficits like balance and auditory overload, and my hope is that, in the next few chapters, you feel inspired to overcome any setbacks, if you put your mind to it and continue trying different methods.

Chapter 6: Exercise

A New Kind of Progress

Known as "The Waco Legend," Michael Johnson was track and field royalty in the 1990s. He was once the fastest man in the world in the two-hundred- and four-hundred-meter race, and won four Olympic gold medals and eight World Championships.

At the time I was writing my book, Michael was recovering from a transient ischemic attack (TIA) or a mini stroke, the extent of which included paralysis on one side of Michael's face and arm, sudden headaches, and slurred speech. TIA usually disappears in a day, but he was still feeling the effects one month later. The *New England Journal of Medicine* published a study stating that a TIA is a warning. In that study, 10 percent of nearly four thousand patients experienced a full-blown stroke within five years. Michael, fifty-one years old at the time, and stroke survivors everywhere, would rather not go down this road.

Why is his story impactful to me? Michael Johnson and I both had a shared

Running a local race in the 90s

interest in running: he as a professional, me as an obsessive enthusiast. Up until our strokes, Michael and I didn't have a history of heart disease. He didn't smoke; I didn't smoke. Michael was working out when he had a stroke; I was running when I had my stroke. The main difference was he had a "mini" stroke, and mine was a clot that turned into a bleed. As a runner, Michael knows that the wins and losses can be measured in hundredths of seconds. Tiny measures matter. Any athlete knows that progress is vital. Michael and I both take pride in our progress post stroke. I'm no local legend, but my stats aren't bad.

Some of my top stats:

YEAR	SPORT	DISTANCE	AGE GROUP	TIME	RANKING
1995	Running US Masters Track & Field Ranking	800 meters	35–39	1:57.7	3rd
1996	Running US Masters Track & Field Ranking	800 meters	35–39	1:58.4	4th
2003	Running Austin's Congress Ave Mile	1 mile	40–44	4:28.8	2nd
2004	Running Austin's Congress Ave Mile	1 mile	40–44	4:31.2	1st

I competed in seventy races in just over fourteen years. The fastest I ever ran, pre-stroke in a 5K was 16:04 minutes, averaging 5:09 per mile. Post stroke, I managed a 15:40 per mile for a 5K.

As a stroke survivor, I can't tell you how frustrating it was for me in the beginning to not find huge strides like I was used to attaining in all of my athletic pursuits. It took me much longer than I expected. I bet people thought I lost hope, but I never gave up

Running the Congress Avenue Mile in 2004, three years before my stroke

on myself or let it bring me down. I was always used to improvement, but now I had to get used to just tiny bits of improvement every day!

The National Stroke Association says that 10 percent of people who have a stroke recover almost completely; 25 percent are left with mild impairments and another 40 percent experience moderate to severe impairments that require special care, like me. I will let you do the math and figure out what happens to the last twenty-five. It is great to be alive!

Research now shows that my brain can somewhat heal itself after a stroke. My cells are damaged, but they will regenerate. It is called neurogenesis. My goal for my personal stroke rehabilitation is to regain a quality of life close to what it was before my stroke. For me,

that means an active and healthy lifestyle, with lots of time for running and biking. I want to live each day to the fullest. George Sheehan, the cardiologist known best for his writings about running, says, "Fitness cannot add to life in the future, but adds to life today." He said that he

Training with Coach Veronica in Austin at the field a few years after my stroke

may not get a long life, but he could certainly get a longer day. I want a longer day, too.

I've mentioned before how I used to set unrealistic recovery goals for myself. It makes me laugh now, to think back when I used to say that I'd be 100 percent back to normal with my walking, running, speech, and life in general a mere five years after my stroke. It's almost hilarious now that so much time has passed, but at the time it was sad to me when I wouldn't achieve my goals. When you don't reach your goals, you feel defeated, like things are just going to end there. But another day comes, and you realize you're still standing, you're blessed to be alive, and you keep pushing towards recovery. Better to keep striving and enjoy the life you have, rather than be miserable about it. If I am truly blessed with longer days, I plan on filling them with running, biking, and working out, regardless of my speed or lack thereof.

Before my stroke, when I would train, occasionally I would hit a plateau. For a time, I would see little advancement or improvement in my running. Co-author of *The Runner's Brain*, Jeffrey L. Brown said, "There's no way around it; plateaus are inevitable and part of the training process. A plateau is rarely permanent. It just indicates what's going on with your training, and perhaps your life, at a particular point in time." In my case, I endured a life change. I had a severe stroke.

About nine months into my post-stroke recovery, I was attending speech, occupational, and physical therapies in Laredo. Right off the bat, I hit a plateau. No progress was happening. Balancing all of the work that my therapists gave me was a disaster. I was *over: over*trained, *over*focused, and *over*whelmed. My mind and body needed just a little interruption. It's hard for anyone to sustain that level of motivation for long, much less a stroke survivor. But I was used to overtraining. Before, even if my coach said to do an easy six miles, I would complete them as fast as I could, with an all-out effort. How quickly I would forget to take care of my body and mind.

As a stroke survivor, I can't afford to forget that. If and when I overtrain, I pay for it. My body is tired for days after, and my aphasia gets even worse. There are ways for me to work on this. I can scale back my target and split my therapies into smaller, more manageable steps. Instead of conquering my speech, occupational, and physical therapies all at once, it's more realistic for me to focus on specific goals that are within reach.

"Develop process goals, not just outcome goals," says Chris Janzen, a mental conditioning coach and founder of TriathleteMind.com. Things like working on my pace, balancing my gait, or mastering running while looking ahead are examples of achievable goals.

Remember when I mentioned that speech therapy is usually only covered a few months after a stroke? The same goes for physical and occupational therapies. Imagine if a survivor is just starting to tackle their process goals, and the insurance runs out and they are sent home. In my case, I knew I could overcome things, but I knew I needed more time. My speech therapist in Laredo, Leslie, another guardian angel, saw this and persuaded the hospital manager to give me six more months of therapies. I pray that all survivors have people like her in their court, to speak up for them. Leslie believing in me helped me feel rejuvenated. I had more mental energy to put into my therapies. Suddenly, I had overcome the plateau in my physical and occupational therapies too.

As an advocate for stroke survivors everywhere, it's important for me to stress that a huge obstacle we face as a group is caps on insurance that were put into place back when it was believed that our brains could not regenerate the cells that are lost post stroke. Now, it has been scientifically proven that cells can be regenerated as long as you keep working on it. Imagine how frustrating that must be when hospital outpatient services discharge you after just three to twelve months of therapy, because that's all insurance will pay for. It takes time. It takes work. It takes patience . . . and it takes creativity on the part of the therapist to try different methods to continue the healing process. You have to be willing to push past the plateau phase.

Overcoming Deficits through Fitness

Rather than letting the disabilities I've suffered stop me, I've let them fuel my fire for recovery. That has led me to network and work with some of the coolest and most patient athletes and trainers in my area and beyond. I've been blessed they will implement any new exercise I want to try; they will do the research to adapt it to my abilities, and they will not let me back down. I can't imagine where I'd be today had it not been for them standing by my side. It wasn't the easiest road to get here, and you can ask any one of my trainers how tough it was at first for us to communicate through the aphasia. I had an agenda and goals, and most of them had never worked with a stroke survivor before. It was a very specific set of needs that we worked on together. Even though I was an athlete, now I was a stroke survivor too. That meant working from square one: teaching my body to walk, and eventually to run again. Things most people take for granted, like simple range of motion, were now an obstacle to tackle on my affected side.

My body maintained posture and circulated blood throughout without any challenges. It was my muscles on the right side of my body that were affected by spasticity. The muscles became stiff and rigid, and simple things like grabbing an apple were no longer possible with my right hand because my fingers would tense up so tight that I couldn't voluntarily open my hand to hold on to things. It took a tremendous amount of strength, from my wife, trainer, or kids, to stretch my fingers open for a split second, before my fist would lock up again. More on this when I talk about my trip to the Taub Clinic.

I suffered from "foot drop" on the right side. My ankle flexion didn't respond as it should when I walked, so that tripped me up often, and on top of that, I had to work on my depth perception since the vision in one eye was also completely gone. Those two things combined made basic walking the first thing I had to overcome. But I wasn't going to stop there.

Training with Coach Veronica

One of my first post-stroke trainers, Coach Veronica Strange, stressed the importance of working the three planes of motion: forward and back, side to side, and rotational. The movements around which she structured my exercises were meant to help reverse the spasticity. They could be swift and energetic, but complex—meaning involving several muscle groups working together. How quick we forget the connection between brain and body, how the brain and muscles must work together as a catalyst to make the body move. For a non-stroke survivor, you'd never even think about the movements you do in just one minute. But a stroke survivor is painfully aware of how many times that system breaks down in those sixty seconds.

Other aspects I really enjoyed about Veronica's workouts were the fact that she made me work out barefoot outside so that I could teach my feet to recruit and wake up the muscles, and she insisted we choose new locations for the workouts often. That meant a unique

More training with Veronica- barefoot is best!

environment each time, which challenged me cognitively. Not only that, she would have me up at the crack of dawn, driving my Smart car through Austin, to find those new places to work out.

Even today, more than fourteen years after the stroke, movement in my weak arm and leg is limited. My proprioception (or the lack of being able to sense the position, location, or the movement of my body) is still off. A few times a week at bedtime, I have tremors in my right leg. My wife helps me stabilize it by putting her leg on top, which helps a little. I guess I owe her since my arm tends to jab at her in the middle of the night as I'm dreaming away. In sickness and in health, right? When I take a run or ride, somewhere along the way, a restraint will affect my body, reducing the chance of success or effectiveness. I strive to find the sense of balance and the sense of movement. But then again, I enjoy the struggle of my race!

A quick side note and message to caregivers and family members of stroke survivors: There will be times that you will want your stroke survivor to take it easy. You will know they are tired mentally and physically. I can no longer count the numerous times my loving and supportive wife begged me to stay home from biking or running when we both knew I was probably overdoing it. The thing is, my competitive nature takes over, and it feels good to let off some steam with a workout. So, instead of forcing your loved one to take it super easy, help them find that balance between not overdoing it, but still finding endorphins. It's a struggle, but you are facing it together, so have patience with them.

In my case, I found Chuck, my trainer, who is also an EMT-paramedic/firefighter. His easy-going personality, balanced with his cautious and skillfully planned workouts, mean I can push myself but my wife can have peace of mind. He and my other trainer, Xavi, give me healthy accountability. Xavi comes up with creative workouts and combines them with the ones I find online. He is a pro at utilizing all of the tools an open gym has to offer us, and we work so many different types of exercises. Things like balance work, agility training, muscle recruitment, and weight-bearing help me work on balancing the strength and mobility in both halves of my body.

Both of them work with me several times a week. Working out with Chuck and Xavi, each new exercise is a new hill to climb. Chuck remembers how in the beginning it was a new challenge for my brain to communicate to the muscles how to move and not fight themselves. We joke now about how he would bring two shirts, because he would have to use his own body to help stabilize me and would get such an intense workout that he'd have to change shirts halfway through. Once we tackled each exercise together, it then became repetition after repetition to become smoother and more efficient so I didn't always need his help. He says it's so important for stroke survivors to have that repetition to try and maintain what you have going and not regress.

Depending on my day at the office or at home, my mind and body will respond differently. Sometimes I just need that little push and the accountability of my trainer to get it going. Other days, my body is just not up for it. I trust their guidance, so on days when they notice I'm off and ask me to stop, I pout, but I stop.

I know not every stroke survivor can afford personal trainers, but the best way to get results is to have a buddy or partner to help you out. With the Laredo Stroke Support Group, we partnered with Enid Vargas at Healthy Physiques, and she guides all of the stroke survivors through total body workouts using different exercise props. She recommends training the whole body instead of just the affected area to achieve optimal strength, balance, and flexibility. Laird Hamilton, one of the greatest surfers, says that it's key to find someone who challenges your weaknesses. That way, they force you to push yourself to do the things you dislike the most, and you get comfortable with the uncomfortable. Most importantly, find another stroke survivor or an athlete that has similar goals and drives you to be your best. Avoid training with someone who has a negative outlook.

One of the key aspects to remember about exercise and physical therapy is that none of us, as survivors, can fit into any box. We all have different needs. Although I was never a big fan of tennis (I'm a ping pong man myself), when Laredo Stroke Support Group partnered with Laredo Tennis Association (LTA) to host biweekly

Survivor, Armando with Tina from LTA

adaptive tennis classes, I knew I wanted to get out there with my stroke buddies. As Tina Trevino, co-founder of LTA, said, "Winning or losing is not a big issue; it's the action." It was another way for us to challenge our brain/body connection and to interact with our stroke peers. I was excited for us to motivate each other, and LTA made it accessible by moving the tennis classes to the racquetball court so we wouldn't have to waste energy chasing after the ball. Other modifications included incorporating slightly smaller-than-adult regulation rackets

Adaptive Tennis Class started out like wall ball

that were a bit lighter and easier to manage,

and low compression balls that bounce a little slower.

When Tina and I reminisce about the journey this program has had, one of the things that we both value is the fact that coaches would interact with stroke survivors as intelligent, high functioning individuals. Sometimes when we go to therapies, we focus on the problem instead of a holistic approach to the whole person. In tennis, we had the opportunity to interact and

communicate with each other in a positive and uplifting way: sharing experiences, playful "trash talk," and lots of fun. Tina remembers how she was touched by a particular survivor's

Tennis is one of the many ways that we come together to stay active and share experiences.

experience; Tony Gonzales not only suffered a stroke, but also had Parkinson's like her late father.

The gift she received from being able to help the survivor flourish with tennis was cathartic. She watched her father slowly lose his ability to play golf, which had been one of his passions. Being able to give all of the participants a second chance at tenacity and a competitive spirit was so rewarding. Tina once shared a study with me where it was documented that one hour a week of physical activity can neurologically bring up your cognitive level, your physical level, your socialization and problem-solving skills, and, most of all, your self-confidence.

Even though the journey is different for every single one of us, physical activity is more valuable than any drug on the market. Beyond just staying in shape and keeping our range of motion so that muscles don't atrophy, quality of life is improved in every aspect thanks to exercise.

My Post-stroke Weekly Workout Plan:

Monday and Wednesday or Friday
- Warm-up walks (lower leg routine twenty steps each): toes, heels, everted, inverted, duck, pigeon
- Neck stretches
- Arm stretches
- Weight bearing (sitting and on ground)
- Martial arts exercise
- Ladder
- BOSU ball
- Stairs
- Rowing machine or Running

Thursday and Saturday
- Biking

Tuesday and Thursday
- Stretch machine
- Warm-up walks (lower leg routine twenty steps each): toes, heels, everted, inverted, duck, pigeon
- Neck and arm stretches
- Weight bearing (sitting and on ground)
- Massage orange ball and roller pin
- Chest fly machine
- Assisted dips and pull-ups
- Leg raises
- "Supermans"

Everyday
- Toes exercises on YouTube
- Neck exercises on YouTube

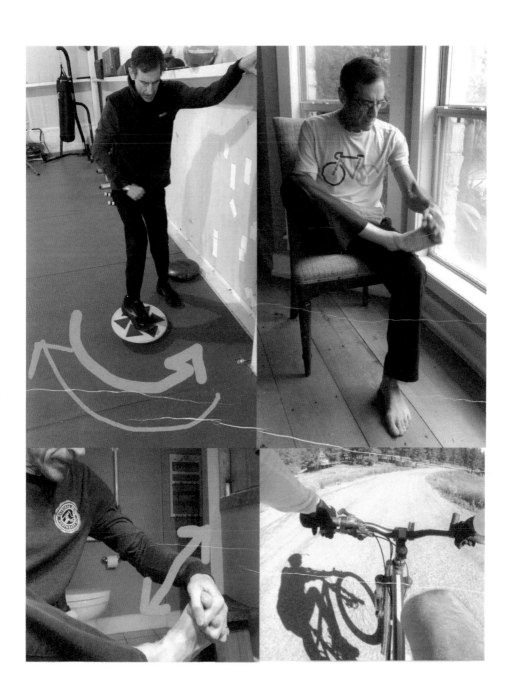

Chapter 7: Non-traditional Approaches

Taub Clinic: Constraint-induced Movement Therapy

Pre-stroke, I exercised with the understanding that the coach is always right, and you get the work done no matter what it takes—no excuses. Post stroke, my approach has changed a bit. Each stroke survivor has to modify the workout to fit their needs. Even still, my competitive side wanted to see results quicker than they were coming, and I was really frustrated not being able to use my right hand. I found a more radical approach to

Wearing my mitt at the Taub Clinic

therapy at the Taub Clinic. The constraint-induced movement therapy program at the University of Alabama approved my application to try a method where you put your dominant, unaffected side in a mitt to force your weaker affected side to become responsive. I expected that, after my stay there, I would return home a new man with 100 percent mobility on my affected side.

My therapist at the clinic, Mary Bowman,

implemented a unique therapy program for a total of three weeks, seven hours a day. It was tough. They used tiresome behavioral training exercises, one-sided training, and work to calm the spasticity in my weak hand. After those rigorous seven hours, I'd go back to the hotel with my wife Deedee to do homework. Lucky for me, she had been a school teacher for thirty-three years, so even though she cringed at the thought of pushing me through the discomfort, she lovingly helped me practice occupational therapy approaches like using my right hand to hold a spoon, putting quarters in the hotel

Practicing using my affected side to eat

washer and dryer, cleaning the table with my weak hand, and pulling back the bedspread. I wore the mitt for 90 percent of the day with the hopes of reversing the deficits.

According to Mary, we were changing my lifestyle by elevating neuroplasticity. I had to understand that my brain change was "use-dependent," meaning that whatever I used my right limbs to do would help rewire those lost parts of my brain. Like a very composed orchestra conductor, Mary guided the slow and controlled movements, and cautioned me against power moves including holding my breath, doing full body muscle contractions, and exerting great effort; they are not helpful in stroke recovery. She mentioned that these strategies tend to stress out the body further. Mind/body fitness through yoga or tai chi can be helpful when working to regain control of the affected limbs. At the Taub Clinic, we used methods like sensory stimulation, positioning and adaptive equipment, and oscillation or swinging and holding the affected elbow higher than your wrist, shaking it side to side. It was enough movement to reset my arm, but not so much that it hurt. Weight-bearing exercises normalized muscle tone, either by activating weak muscles or reigning in overactive ones. These therapies activate more awareness of each limb and remind the brain to rely on them for supporting the body and for participating in everyday life.

Therapist, Mary Bowman, Deedee & I

Deedee and I enjoyed Mary's methods, and we loved her company even more. Mary's catchphrases like "Use it or lose it!" and

Sitting outside the Taub Clinic

"That brilliant and wonderful brain" will forever be in our memories of the Taub Clinic. One not-so-wonderful memory is the ice baths. I'm a pretty tough guy, but dumping my right arm into the excruciating ice bath made me cry on the inside! It was just a short thirty seconds at a time, but I swear it felt like thirty minutes. We continued those ice baths for about a year-and-a-half after the clinic, to help relax my hand before doing weight-bearing exercises.

My least favorite part of therapy was the ice baths

Closing that chapter in recovery, it was tough to come home unable to fully rely on my right arm and hand. I did, however, gain a sense of grip in my fingers. It gave me the confidence I needed to ride my bike and workout with gym equipment again, and I even began trying some aqua strength pool workouts.

Muscle engagement on the affected side means hope!

Ruthe B. Cowl Rehabilitation Center (RBC)

A few weeks after my return home, I felt it was important to continue the exercises and therapy I had learned at the Taub Clinic. I searched for a local resource and came across Ruthe B. Cowl Rehabilitation Center. Founded by an amazing woman, her dream was to improve quality of life for those with stroke or brain injuries and other physical conditions.

Even though their program is very thorough for most survivors, I like to push the envelope. I shared some of the Taub Clinic's Constraint Induced therapy methods, and they were more than willing to help me stay on track. I was blessed to have the support of their team and continued physical and

Therapist, Roxy, overseeing my work with the Alter G.

occupational therapy at Ruthe B. Cowl for about two years. One of the most innovative and fun therapies they offered during my time there was the Alter G Anti-Gravity Treadmill which uses NASA Differential Air Pressure technology to allow patients to move without pain and recover mobility. I certainly felt like an astronaut as I ran with the support of the machine.

Believe it or not, one of the simplest devices that offered me a substantial amount of help with my balance was the parallel bars. As a survivor, my affected side often would get left behind as I would walk or exercise. Even just walking in the warehouse at my business, I would walk in a diagonal line when trying to walk straight. Those parallel bars gave me feedback and helped me walk straighter. It's crazy to think that as much as I wanted to tackle huge feats like running again, I was still working on things like eating with a spoon and walking a straight line.

Parallel Bar work at Ruthe B. Cowl

Perla Johnson and I working on mobility in my right arm and hand.

My Occupational Therapist: Bob Whitford

About two years into my stroke recovery at Saint David's Hospital, I met a beast on a bike, therapist Bob Whitford. It was still very early on the road to recover my range of motion. My brother-in-law lent me his

I'm continuously amazed at how Bob balances with one arm on the bike.

115

recumbent bike in an attempt to get me back into action. Though I missed my mountain bike, I invested in my own recumbent and was determined to go biking or triking regularly.

The joy of biking outdoors lasted for about three months, until I really started to miss the adrenaline of a mountain bike. I imagine it probably matched the adrenaline of my wife watching me pedal four or five feet across the yard and wiping out immediately. She'd help me try to get on my bike, which was a task in itself, and then tears would well up as she watched me wipe out and joke about it. I was determined to make it happen, regardless. Casually talking with Amy, an occupational therapist at Saint David's, I mentioned how much I missed it, and the struggles I was facing. She insisted, "You've got to meet Bob!" Like Amy, Bob Whitford is an occupational therapist.

Since Bob lost his arm at a very young age, he anticipated my needs very well. Despite this impairment, he went on to conquer so much with his bike, and from 1996 to 2002, he competed as a Paralympian in Atlanta and Sydney. Once Bob retired from that level of cycling, he decided to share his passion with others, to help them on their journey towards recovery. "There is something about a life-changing injury that kind of lets you speak to each other at a different level. It creates a heightened sense of interaction between individuals, and allows you to communicate your needs better," said Whitford.

In my case, Bob implemented one-legged pedaling drills on the stationary trainer with the strong leg supported and the weak leg doing all of the pedaling. We only met one day a week, but we made the most of it. After a few months, and once Bob

Survivor Armando watches as Bob takes his bike off of his motorcycle.

thought I was ready, we transitioned outside. It took me by surprise when he said, "Let's go," and took me out to the sidewalk at Saint David's to practice. It was buzzing with people and was as narrow as could be. I should have been nervous and distracted, but I was thrilled! I dominated the sidewalk and faced my fears, with Bob alongside me. His inspirational story motivated me, and he loved the quote, "Four wheels move the body, but two wheels move the soul."

The Progression of a Stroke Survivor's Ride by Bob Whitford:

1. Adapted tricycle or recumbent

2. One-legged pedaling drill for the affected leg: balance, cognitive, and reaction speeds are safe and fast enough

3. Adapted pedal systems: a lock-in pedal for the weak leg strap or a specialty shoe platform

4. Mounting the bike

5. Dismounting from the bike

6. Hip rotation to disengage from the weak leg

7. Straddling the bike and laying the bike down

8. Stepping over the frame

LSSG Riders, at different points in their Ride Progression

My Chiropractors: Dr. Brian Drake and Dr. Cason Davis

I consider it a blessing that, despite adversity in my life, I maintain a positive outlook. Naturally, I choose to surround myself with others that vibrate on a higher frequency.

Right around the same time that I was working with Bob, I was attending speech therapy at ASL (Austin Speech Labs), which is where I met David Little, a stroke survivor. Even though it took me a while to get to know David, we got to talking about his

David & I at one of our first sessions with Dr. Drake

chiropractor and the strides he was making towards balancing out his body post stroke. He recommended Dr. Bryan Drake, and I had no idea what I was signing up for.

Here's how I describe the methods he used to train David and me: a little bit of madness and a little bit of magic. He designed an obstacle course for us using a railroad track, a parking lot curb, and stairs to challenge us in new ways, so our

Dr. Drake exercising and isolating my affected side

bodies could fight back to recover lost balance and mobility. Most importantly, I think he wanted us to overcome mental blocks and fear of falling. David and I worked tirelessly to perform each assigned task.

Thinking outside the box & overcoming mental blocks

When I think back now, I get nostalgic because it was such a gift the doctor gave us. Instead of just giving us a chiropractic adjustment, he dedicated time to doing something really different. We worked together for a short period of time before he moved out of town. His successor, Dr. Cason Davis, had big shoes to fill . . . and he did.

Even though it was the first time he worked with stroke survivors, he was inspired by what Dr. Drake started. Dr. Davis says he loved being able to help us as patients beyond what regular physical therapy would usually offer. Most patients get "Do this motion ten times for three sets," etc., repetitive monotonous exercises. Even though that approach has merit, when a survivor gets back home, they are usually limited to just the type of motion practiced. Here, he had given us functional fitness to take with us through life. Dr. Davis mentioned he had only been out of school for a couple of years, so it was overwhelming to work with us at first and he wondered how effective he would be. He built on Dr. Drake's treatments and brought his own unique skills to the table, like the myofascial release technique called ART (active release technique) that did wonders for David and me. He described that it just makes sense: if we do not use our muscles as they are designed to be used, after some time, they begin to atrophy. "They begin to lose their strength and develop adhesions from not being put through the whole range of motion the way they should."

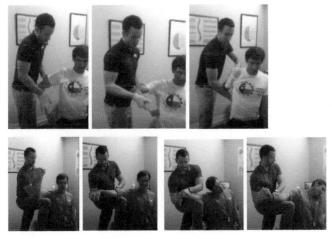

Working with Dr. Davis & ART

ART breaks up the adhesions so your muscles, joints, and nerves can return to their original range of motion. I had forgotten the drastic changes we would see from the moment we walked in to ten minutes later. It was impressive and left me hopeful when I saw the muscles move freely again, even for just a little while afterwards, before they would stiffen up again.

Korean Martial Arts: Master Lee

Of all the things Dr. Drake taught us, he strongly advocated that we seek out a martial arts outlet to work the brain/body connection. I took out my phone, Googled "martial arts," and found a place just a few blocks away. When I walked in and met Master Lee, his

Master Lee & I

huge smile was very inviting. And it turned out he had trained another stroke survivor, so he had a few ideas for where to start with me. Master Lee didn't speak much English, but his kind wife was our translator. She had to deal with my aphasia, plus a language barrier between us. Talk about being patient.

A world-class martial artist with over thirty-five years of experience, he had been in over three hundred martial arts demonstrations worldwide. Master Lee taught unarmed combat for five years to the Korean Military Police. Who knew he'd be a godsend for a stroke survivor from Laredo like me?

Master Lee taught me things like diaphragmatic breathing and other forms of breath control. Even though one side of my body was very tight, he wanted us to work on controlling the movements to even out both sides. One of

Working hard together

my favorite exercises that I still practice includes a sit-up with arms extended overhead. The tricky part is holding a broomstick to even out my hands, and then adding some more weight by pressing down while trying to sit up. He would guide the move, while weighing it down even more. No mercy for a stroke survivor willing to put in the work. Another exercise we call the "hai- hai-hai" continues to be a great way to challenge body halves. It involves a hook with one arm, a hook with the other, then a knee jab with one side, and then repeating the same on the other side.

What seems like a simple move to someone else is so tough when one side of your body just doesn't respond the same way.

It takes a lot to balance, to avoid falling, and to remember which side is next. So, it's a mental challenge as much as a physical challenge. After just six reps or so, my affected leg starts to become so heavy I have to stop and take a break or I risk falling back, though don't ask me to admit that in front of my gym friends.

Institute of Functional Rehabilitation and Exercise

After my stroke, I read a really cool manual called "The Successful Stroke Survivor." Author Tom Balchin developed a unique rehabilitation program, after surviving a stroke at age twenty-one. I was so inspired, I sent him several emails in one week, and before waiting for a response, I just picked up the phone and called him. The excitement to finally reach him certainly amped up my aphasia during that phone call. He was very understanding and patient, and after hearing my stroke story, he quickly invited me to visit the Institute of Functional Rehabilitation and Exercise.

Located in England, the institute trains therapists to teach stroke survivors how to fall. No, that's not a typo. They teach us how to fall safely so that we are prepared and avoid further injuries. I had the opportunity to participate in a training almost exclusively for therapists. Myself and one other stroke survivor practiced falling down and learning how to get up on our own, alongside about fifteen therapists. We were empowered with the knowledge and tools to share with our stroke buddies.

I got back to Laredo proud to teach our Laredo Stroke Support Group, with the help of our group trainer Enid. Tom's method is another tool in our toolbelt to overcome daily obstacles as a survivor. I highly recommend every stroke survivor study that manual and learn how to fall safely, amongst other things.

Practicing how to fall safely with LSSG, after my trip to London

They say if you fall down seven times, you stand up eight. Even with years of practice, life loves to throw curveballs. I'd think about Tom's manual again when Deedee and I took a trip to visit David, a close friend who had suffered a stroke. It was freezing, so we were rushing to see him and struggled to find the right building at Baylor Hospital. My hands were stuck inside my jacket pockets, and I

The calm after the storm

was jogging to get out of the cold wind. Suddenly I was attacked by the sidewalk. A little bitty half-inch sliver of sidewalk clipped my right shoe and brought me down. It was like a slow-motion video starring me! My face hit the sidewalk, but not before my glasses did a number on my nose. I'd end up as a patient in the hospital, before I'd be a visitor.

I still can't believe with all of the therapies, weight-bearing exercises, traveling with friends, and "how to fall" manual, I was in that moment. Nothing prepares you for every single element like weather, hands in your pockets, falling face first . . . Each situation is unique. You can't always prepare. Even having the knowledge of how to fall correctly, in the moment, it's hard to adapt and apply what you know. I was trying to get up, but feeling very dizzy. My ego said, "You're twenty-seven years old," but my aching head said, "You're sixty." It was a great lesson in patience.

Chapter 8: Diet and Nutrition

When my grandmother was a young lady, she went to the University of the Incarnate Word in San Antonio,  Texas. She was a boarder there, so all her meals were prepared on site. The nuns of Incarnate Word made the students eat vegetables every day. All throughout my grandparents' lives, they grew vegetables and fruits. They passed that tradition on to my mom, but it took me a while to come around.

My grandfather & my mom

I was the youngest of four kids. Throughout pre-college, I did really well in school, football, basketball, baseball, and track. Thanks to genetics and being extremely active, I was always thin and lanky, regardless of what I ate. Even though I ate plenty of vegetables in my diet at home, I also loved candy like Tootsie Rolls, Pixy Stix, and Bit-O-Honey bars, just to name a few.

It's not like I was completely clueless to what a balanced meal should have been. I remember in high school, the American food pyramid contained four main food groups: milk, meat, fruit and vegetables, and bread and cereals. In the 1990s, they added an unhealthy food group that included alcoholic beverages, refined sugar, and fats. Somehow, it still didn't seem important enough to me to make healthier, more balanced choices. So, I ate what I enjoyed versus what I thought was healthy. My normal lunch was a typical Mexican plate in a restaurant: enchiladas, beans and rice with a side of guacamole, and a tall glass of iced tea. The ingredients were to die for—literally! The only healthy thing on my plate was the guacamole or avocado.

By the time I turned forty, I still did not realize my health had everything to do with my diet. The older I get, my nutrition choices are led by my desire to stave off the world's leading killers like cancer, heart attack, and stroke. Now my diet includes foods like carrots, kale, spinach, and many other plant-based foods that incorporate vitamins (A, E, D, and K) and fish, eggs, avocado, and extra-virgin olive oil to protect my body and my brain against another stroke and aging.

Refined Sugar and Caffeine

For me, a typical pre-stroke work week consisted of drinking three cans of Dr Pepper before lunch to cope with the stress of managing a moving and storage company. I wore many hats throughout the day and had to have answers for everything and everyone, all day long. I needed to hydrate my body and my brain, but I didn't want water. I wanted to be "on" at all times, ready to react and be alert. Dr Pepper was a quick fix, because it would amp me up, but the problem was the crash that followed a few hours later. The simple carbohydrates, aka refined sugars, in caffeinated beverages do cause fatigue. Refined sugar is extremely addictive, similar to cigarettes and alcohol. The American Heart Association states men should not consume more than nine teaspoons of refined sugar daily, and for women it is only six. But the USDA affirms that Americans enjoy twenty-two teaspoons per day—twenty-two! We are hooked on that sweet stuff that causes high blood sugar or hyperglycemia, and it is connected with inflammatory diseases. I'm on the other side now and haven't had a soda since 2012, and I'm not looking back.

Alcohol

In the latter part of 2011, I read *Making a Good Brain Great* by Daniel Amen, MD. In his book, he scanned an eighty-two-year-old woman's brain, which revealed she had one of the healthiest brains. In another picture, he scanned a young male who was a moderate drinker. His brain scan reminded me of a road full of potholes! Those potholes represented the damage alcohol created.

The book impacted me so much that the next time I joined a colleague for a beer, after just two, I felt so guilty because I knew the damage I could potentially do to my brain. If I truly want my brain to be like that eighty-two-year-old lady's, drinking is no longer an option.

There is *always* the risk of a repeat stroke with me, and alcohol does things to our brain that can affect the way it works. It makes it harder to think clearly and move with coordination. Alcohol is a diuretic, and my body would be losing more fluid than it takes in; on top of that, I suffer from heartburn, and alcohol intensifies this discomfort.

Basic H_2O

I'm a stroke survivor, and if only in my mind, I will always be an endurance athlete. Hydration is key for optimal performance. My daily performance now consists of talking to my customers or my employees at work, as well as exercises like biking or running. I pay a big price if I'm even the slightest bit dehydrated. Water is extremely important to me now!

As a stroke survivor and an athlete, I am grateful for this awareness. Monique Ryan, author of *Sports Nutrition for Endurance Athletes*, says, "Clean and calorie-free water is basic and natural." Don't take basic water for granted.

I start my day with hydration in mind. I drink twelve ounces or more of water. Throughout the entire day, I carry water with me at all times.

Diet

For the past ten years, I've been on a quest for the most balanced, optimal diet, one that makes me feel great and makes my body work well. I keep gravitating to the Mediterranean diet because it incorporates the most whole foods. I also love the mantra, "Eat food. Not too much. Mostly plants," written by Michael Pollan in his book *In Defense of Food: An Eater's Manifesto*. Many scientific organizations support healthy changes to a lifestyle, like that of the Mediterranean diet, for preventing medical illnesses or diseases. The diet draws attention to—ready or not—eating plant-based foods, no butter (I use olive oil), more herbs and spices (a tiny bit of sea salt), and fish and poultry.

Nevertheless, I'm in Laredo and I'm surrounded by Mexican restaurants and billboards with fajita tacos paired with giant sodas. Take, in particular, just the members of the Laredo Stroke Support Group (LSSG). We are 98.5 percent Mexican American. Flour tortillas and guisado de carne are the number one and two things we're craving! At our first few LSSG meetings, we got laughed at and had tons of leftovers when we passed out a healthy quinoa salad for snack. We understand now that we have to encourage healthier choices on a much smaller scale and appropriate to the culture we live in. Even though it is natural to want to enforce a strict diet for our group, we must excite them about healthy choices that taste good first, and then make our way to the more unique options.

Personally, I have come so far on my nutrition journey. I eat very clean, whole foods now. My body thrives when I regularly consume food like fruits, vegetables, protein-rich animal and plant foods, nuts, almond milk, and nonfat yogurt. You can never go wrong eating antioxidant-rich foods like vegetables, fruits, and whole grains. They protect cells from the damage caused by free radicals, and prevent disease. Researchers also say eating almonds can lower my risk of gum disease and bad breath, by almost 30 percent, so I sneak those in too for an occasional snack.

Dr. Don Colbert, author of *Let Food Be Your Medicine*, suggests we need to treat the root of medical issues, not the symptoms. Inflammation is the root cause of most chronic diseases. Trauma, like my stroke, can flip a switch in our bodies that makes us susceptible to inflammation and, thus, auto-immune diseases.

Hippocrates said, "Let food be thy medicine and medicine be thy food." So whatever diet path you choose to support your health, strive for eating whole foods and things that limit inflammation. As a stroke survivor, I now know my gut has a direct connection with my brain's performance and suggest you get your gut in gear. Making healthy changes to your diet can help battle forgetfulness, depression, anxiety, anger, and most importantly inflammation.

Chapter 9: The New Human

The Amen Clinic Epiphany

In the fall of 2011, it was time for my yearly check up with Dr. Godines. He recommended a book he was reading by Dr. Daniel G. Amen. He said I would like the book

The book that piqued my curiosity for improving my brain's functioning

because a lot of what it covered pertained to stroke. *Making A Good Brain Great* took a long time for me to read back then, because my aphasia was putting up a barricade of sorts. It took me almost a whole year to finish the book, but I was so inspired that eventually Deedee and I flew to California, to the Amen Clinic, to apply the new technology he speaks about in his book. This was six years after my stroke. Dr. Amen is the founder of eight nationally recognized outpatient healthcare clinics focused on improving mental health. Specifically, I was very interested in their procedure called neuroimaging. Dr. Amen has thirty years of experience taking SPECT scans (an acronym for single-photon emission computerized tomography).

The initial four-hour consultation was grueling for me because half of my brain was severely lagging behind. As stroke survivors, our brains need longer processing times to listen to the question, think about the answer, and then actually get it out for others to hear. On top of that, because I was so excited to actually be there experiencing it all, my aphasia really kicked in and my wife had to help me communicate my answers. As you can imagine with any marriage, the answer in my brain didn't always match my wife's answer for me. After an exhausting four hours, it was on to the neuropsychological testing. The final day was reserved for brain SPECT imaging and lab tests with the psychiatrist, Dr. Darmal.

Deedee felt the main benefit of our trip to Amen Clinic and receiving the SPECT scan was that I could now get a tangible picture of my brain that showed the insult that occurred with my stroke. I saw the part that was inactive as a blank on the screen. It made me realize there was a lot to work on and recovery would take longer than I had originally expected. Remember

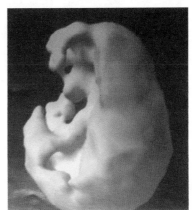

Humbling view of my brain's SPECT scan

when I reflected on how adversity builds character? Sitting there at the clinic, I saw my expectation of running and speaking normally by next year fly out the window. Guess this was one of those defining moments where I could choose to play the victim or the survivor.

The report said, "Bill exhibits excessive as well as deficient phase statistics, meaning his [brain] is not working at peak efficiency." You'd better believe that I was going to work as hard as I could to get my brain back in tip-top shape.

Fast-forward twelve years, after many therapy sessions, workouts, and rehab visits, I flew back to California to see Dr. Larry Momaya at the Amen Clinic, following my own recommendation and wish for a twelve-year follow up. They had me wait around for about an hour-and-a-half with about four or five other patients in the waiting room. I was sitting on pins and needles, wondering whether or not the scan would show an improvement in my left hemisphere. This waiting made my right hemisphere work overtime. When the scan was done, Dr. Momaya said, "Not going to sugarcoat it; your left brain is bad!"

Much to my initial disappointment, my left brain was still falling short, but he explained that my body was recruiting my right hemisphere where it needed to, and that was okay, too. Yet another important lesson in patience.

Strokefocus

Years ago, Laredo Stroke Support Group and I were invited to participate in an exciting project known as Strokefocus. Its vision is "Stroke can be cured. Make it a reality sooner."

We know every great medical breakthrough includes two indispensable components:

1. A breakthrough idea

2. Millions of trials and errors to test out the idea, to become a clinical reality accessible by the average person

Stroke survivors everywhere will be relieved to know that a breakthrough idea is already being tested. In 2016, a neurosurgery team at Stanford University discovered that, after stroke, brain circuits just go dormant. They don't actually die as we thought before. They are testing ways to inject adult stem cells, converted from an adult's own bone marrow, into the brain to bring the circuits back to life.

Strokefocus Project sees a wide opening in part two. There are survivors eager to participate. The challenge is they do not have an organized way to discover research projects or be discovered by researchers. Local support organizations are also struggling to keep survivors who want to participate. In the case of Laredo Stroke Support Group, it has taken several years for us to figure out the right type of activities that entice survivors, but most importantly, the right approach to get them to actually attend meetings or become part of the group. This is mostly due to the fact that, once they are discharged from the hospital and realize their life is changed forever, they get depressed. Our goal is to help them connect, learn, and recover with other survivors so their quality of life can be great again. Imagine if we could collectively work to help find a cure.

Strokefocus reminded us how important just one tiny medical discovery can be for our entire future. They described that penicillin was discovered in 1929. By the 1940s, the United States could only make enough to treat ten adults per year. Fast forward to the 1960s, and every soldier in Normandy had access, and any patient with pneumonia was no longer fatal. What a concept for stroke recovery. The crazy part is that the cure to stroke is the same as for traumatic brain injury. So, when you put those two groups of patients together, you're talking about a huge impact on our society's recovery and money spent on things like veteran long-term disability, rehab after stroke, etc. Imagine if we could fast track those forty years of testing by supporting things like Stanford's discovery, with more testing, sooner.

I have hope for the near future when a cure will come. In the meantime, other trials have proven successful, like at Harborview University Hospital in Seattle, Washington.

Thrombectomies
In mid-September 2019, we were invited by Dr. Melanie Walker, an endovascular neurosurgeon, to Harborview University Hospital in Seattle, Washington, to observe a removal of an aneurysm. Dr. Walker talked us through the entire surgery explaining step by step what we were seeing on the screens. The most fascinating thing was the fact that they had made a small incision in the patient's groin area to work up through the vein and through her carotid artery in her neck to the aneurysm. It was so exciting that they did not have to open her up or drill through her skull for the surgery, like they did with me. We watched as they inserted a coil into the

aneurysm, and added a stent. It was so amazing! All of this thanks to advancements in technology.

We did not get to see a stroke surgery, but they explained they are able to do similar surgeries the same way. They can go through the person's wrist or groin area. The important thing is that, if the person arrives within twenty-four hours of their stroke, they can usually reverse the deficits of the stroke. *Reverse the deficits of the stroke*—it's mind-blowing! The patient we saw was able to speak to us after her surgery, as if nothing had happened.

"I wish I knew what the future holds in this field," said Dr. Melanie Walker, the endovascular neurosurgeon. When I interviewed her, she said, "Feels like it's all happening so quickly! Science moves slowly, so this is a real treat to see." Endovascular approaches to stroke recovery already existed, but in 2017, all the clinical trials demonstrated truly magical effects so now it really has become

Some of the team at Harborview University Hospital, with Dr. Melanie Walker 2nd to the right

the standard of care. They do thrombectomies up to twenty-four hours after stroke, and sometimes even longer if there is tissue to save and they can get to it safely. Compare that with my stroke and how much brain function I lost. I wish I had a time machine and a rocket ship to fly me to Seattle the day of my stroke. We'd be having a different conversation.

Here's the catch: To become a neurovascular surgeon, it can take up to twenty years of schooling, and the field is still very small. The doctors trained to do this kind of procedure are already spread thin, so if you're looking for a unique degree to pursue, here's your opportunity to change the world!

After witnessing two surgeries, we visited with the stroke coordinator at the hospital. They have so much to offer in their hospital because of their location and the number of patients they treat. She commended the efforts of Laredo Stroke Support Group and commented that we are ahead of most support groups that she has seen or heard about. Hearing that made us want to continue to work with Strokefocus to share our group's format with other places (even if just to surrounding cities and states), especially when we think back to where we were the weeks after my stroke, when we couldn't find a support group or any starting point. We'd love to provide that security and guidance for others at this point.

The Decade of the Brain
In 1990, President George H. W. Bush announced the "Decade of the Brain." For the next ten years, it was decided that brain research would be brought to the forefront in the United States. To demonstrate how quickly research can impact us as a society, here are five of the outcomes from that decade, published in an article on scientificamerican.com, that I find to be most relevant in regards to stroke:

1. Neurogenetics: The quick identification of clusters of disease-related genes will help us identify and treat brain disorders.

2. Brain mapping: This tells us not only where specific genes are active, but also how these circuits process the flow of information to the brain.

3. The malleable brain: Where we once thought the brain was malleable in infancy but resistant to change thereafter, now we acknowledge and exploit adult plasticity.

4. Optogenetics: Understanding how various networks of neurons contribute to behavior, perception, and cognition allows us to decipher how various brain cells elicit feelings, thoughts, and movements, and how they can go awry.

5. Neural implants: These can now be implanted in the brain to restore lost function.

Each of these findings will have immense contribution in the prevention, detection, and cure for stroke in the next decade.

One of the angels throughout my recovery has been my neurologist, Dr. Fernando Sanchez. We have a standing date every Thursday at 5:00 p.m., where we go bike riding on one of our favorite hilly trails. I enjoy spending time with him because he always teaches me something new about the brain. On one of our more recent visits, I asked him what he saw on

Dr. Sanchez & I at the LSSG Hope Rocks Gala

the horizon in regards to stroke and the brain, and he was more than happy to share his insights. Primarily, he believes that health care and self-care will be significantly altered by new technologies and the implementation of artificial intelligence. Since there are many diseases that affect our nervous system, lots of important research has been done and the nervous system is what he predicts to be impacted the most by these changes. The way things are tracking, in the next thirty years, instead of current biological methods like a peel or injection to modify the way the cells function in our brains, we will see the implementation of some type of computer interface. It will be something like a computer chip, similar to the ones we insert in our cell phones, and the coolest part is that this would allow us to enhance or suppress a particular brain function. What does that mean for someone like me? In the case of my aphasia, it would allow me to reconnect the missing paths in my brain to help with my speech. In the case of my affected side, my right arm and leg would reconnect to my brain and would respond when a desired movement is delegated to them.

I thought it was interesting when he mentioned that this is already being tested in animals with success. But it's currently impractical to operate and share this with all of the stroke survivors, Alzheimer patients, and other patients impacted by neurological diseases. That brought me back to what Strokefocus has set out to do: link survivors and researchers. If the technology already exists, but all that is missing is the clinical trials, I say, "Sign me up today." Still, I'm hopeful and excited for future stroke survivors to have that technology at their disposal, though I'm a little jealous that my stroke friends and I can't benefit from it today.

Dr. Sanchez says humans used to be dependent on evolution, but now it seems crazy to think we are driving our own evolution. Things like this wouldn't be possible without the years of research to uncover misconceptions like the fact that we thought brain plasticity was only possible in infants and small children, and now we know it takes work and time, but it can be modified in adults too. Furthermore, he explained to me that transhumanism or "becoming more than human" is closer than we think. Things like nanotechnology, allowing us to make use of artificial robotic limbs, will be life-changing for stroke survivors. How cool would I look with a bionic arm and leg? Dr. Sanchez says we should be prepared for the new human.

Speaking of the new human, flashing back to about ten years ago when I first started working with Dr. Urquidez in Austin, he introduced me to a man named Matt Rigby. Little did I know that Matt and I would become great friends. A champion for individuals who have neurological deficits and pain, Matt works as the vice president of business development for a company called Bioness in the United States. As an occupational therapist, Matt practiced for

Matt staying active and appreciating the outdoors

several years, but eventually was drawn to the commercial side of things when he discovered there were products and resources that could help others—things he would have used in his clinical practice—but not enough people that knew about them.

Even though there are so many different types of therapy devices, when Matt talks about how Bioness is raising the bar in the industry, it gives me hope. He says there has been a lot of research in the past ten years that has shown "the most critical piece of a system that provides support to someone to learn how to walk is that that system allows someone to walk over normal ground to get normal schematics or ground reaction forces."

Normal treadmills don't do that, since the person is walking in response to the movement of the treadmill, and not their own cadence.

Right off the bat, Matt suggested I try out the L300 on my right leg. Dr. U didn't want to brace my leg because that would do the work for me. Instead, he wanted me to train my body to walk again, and eventually to run. The L300 would send electrical impulses from my brain to my spinal cord, and continue to stimulate the particular muscle until it learned how to perform on its own. In particular, I struggled with foot drop, and because the front toes would droop down, my right leg would often trip me up. On top of that, because of the stroke in my eye, my depth perception was off. So, you could imagine how important it was for me to regain this basic movement so I wouldn't be at risk of falling on a daily basis.

Matt and the team at Bioness understand one of the biggest fears of stroke survivors is falling. This probably stems from the fact that most therapists will focus much of therapy on avoiding the fall. Falling equals getting injured. But Matt says, "When we prevent you from falling, we are preventing you from learning how to move normally and react to things that cause you to fall: curves, uneven surfaces, gravel, things that you might encounter in the real world. So the reality is counter-intuitive. We want to allow you to fall. We want you to learn in therapy. Because you learn from that."

One of their more recent products, The Vector, introduces a new kind of training that provides the safety of a static system, but also the range of motion and retraining of a dynamic system. It has the added advantage of making you feel safe enough to fall, since it can limit how fast and how far you fall. When it comes to therapy, it gives you the validation of knowing how your body is responding and how effectively the therapy is working. You can actually track the mobility changes, so it all goes back to us working with technology to create the "new human." I love the fact that, instead of feeling like we have to stay in a protective bubble all of the time, worried about falling, we will now have the confidence to train a little harder and step out of our comfort zone. How else will we know what our brain and our body are capable of in terms of recovery?

Visualization & Hypnosis

You may have heard the saying, "When the student is ready, the teacher will appear." I can count on one hand the times in my life hypnosis and meditation have been introduced to me and the times that I was intrigued, but ultimately didn't pay them much attention. As someone who is always on the go, without much down time for contemplation or relaxation, I always assumed that

Recent video chat with Peter, discussing the benefits of visualization and eliciting positive emotions for stroke survivors

meditation was a waste of time. It wasn't until about thirteen years ago when I was grasping for anything to help me overcome the effects of my stroke that I debated actually trying hypnosis. When I searched the Internet for a specialist somewhere nearby, I was shocked to see that there was actually a hypnotherapist in Laredo.

Peter Kingsley, originally from Birmingham, England, met with me throughout the course of a year. It wasn't until a few sessions in that I learned he was a professional athlete back home, and of course that helped me relate to him even more. He said, as an athlete, he knew and developed his mindset to the point where he was able to do amazing things in his career.

To be clear, my goal for incorporating hypnosis was to be able to access the parts of my brain that were blocked, specifically relating to my range of motion in both halves of my body. During our sessions, Peter asked me to visualize going through the motions of certain activities using both arms and legs. He always emphasized that the first step was learning to mentally relax. So, he'd ask me questions about things that elicited positive emotions like joy, peace, happiness, and most importantly pleasure. That helped us custom-build my visualization. We included things like biking in the California Redwood Forest, my favorite color orange, playing baseball and football on the beach, and writing the names of five friends on the wet sand.

Peter asked me to repeat this exact visualization before bed each night to relax my mind and help me fall asleep. He said that even though the exact details are important to me, as my guide, he was more about tuning into those specific emotions (how you feel versus what you think) to know what works to help me relax.

Peter explained it to me like this:

Step 1: Prep—learn the skill to mentally relax.

Step 2: Train/Learn—program for training with mental relaxation and be consistent.

Step 3: Perform—use the talent that you've gained.

I have definitely incorporated that into my daily workouts. If I do not mentally relax beforehand, my spasticity goes haywire and I do not have a productive or enjoyable workout session. My trainers Chuck and Xavi will be the first to tell me, "Bill, you're having on off day," and they'll help me rethink our workout with something simpler for my mind.

This approach has also advanced my public speaking. Earlier when preparing for a big speech, I'd mentally relax and meditate, practice giving the speech for hours, and then eventually perform it. The same holds true even now. If I don't have time to relax my mind before, my aphasia kicks in and holds my words hostage.

Almost a decade later, researching about hypnosis and meditation and the benefits they can offer stroke survivors, I came across an article regarding the prefrontal cortex, calling it "the brain's control panel." My mind was blown. Peter had used the example of when we want to look something up on the Internet, the tool we use is a computer. If we want to access parts of our mind, a tool we can use is hypnosis or meditation. So, when I read this article and it explained that not many of us have control of our control panel, it just made sense.

For many stroke survivors, the control panel has malfunctioned. Here are the four main ways that meditation and hypnosis can reset our control panel.

1. Activate and thicken the prefrontal cortex: Relaxation through meditation and hypnosis increases gray matter density in parts of the brain that plan, make decisions, solve problems, and regulate emotion.

2. Strengthens connection of prefrontal cortex and amygdala: Meditation and hypnosis can help moderate emotional responses, help with patience, calmness, and resilience—a huge area where stroke survivors can benefit.

3. Prevents the prefrontal cortex from shrinking: Meditators who were fifty years old

had the same gray matter in the prefrontal cortex as twenty-five-year-olds.

4. Increases activity in the left prefrontal cortex, which is associated with happiness: T Meditation and hypnosis help prevent depression for stroke survivors by keeping their brain active.

If meditation and hypnosis are not currently something you're familiar with, a more accessible approach would be to learn how to self-talk. Much like a runner on the last mile of a race learns to coach his mind to finish strong, as a survivor, you must coach yourself daily. When you're trying to have a conversation and your aphasia kicks in, for example, you can coach yourself positively with phrases like, "Speak a little slower. You can do this. Take your time."

Stroke survivor and author Alison Shapiro writes in her book *Healing into Possibility*, "Our brains are expensive real estate and when we leave them vacant it's wasteful." That really hit home. I can't imagine God put me on this earth to have a stroke at age forty-seven and for me to waste away and die. I believe I'm still young and have a lot to contribute before I get to heaven.

If I'm going to rewire my brain so I can continue to be mentally strong, then I'll have to reach in to my playbook and pull out some of the plays that helped me throughout my life.

Epilogue: My Go-To Plays

Don't multitask. Instead, be in the moment.

Practice mental relaxation often. Like a control panel that has been reset, this allows your body and mind to perform optimally.

Stay positive. No matter what you're going through, a positive mindset will keep you motivated to change your circumstances for the better.

Practice self-talk. Repeat key statements to yourself to keep your eye on the task at hand.

Get support. Having accountability buddies keeps you on track.

Put in the effort. Others can motivate you, but it's up to you to show up and do the work.

For me, the hardest part about writing this book was trying to organize all of the transformative experiences and mind-blowing conversations I've had, which have led me to where I am today on my journey to stroke recovery. There have been so many amazing people that have given me insight, have lent a hand, have offered their support and encouragement, and I wouldn't be where I am without their inspirational example.

For my epilogue, I thought you should meet these key players that were always on my team, and as you read through them, I ask you to pay close attention to the diversity you'll see—stroke doesn't discriminate. From their previous profession, to the extent of their recovery, to their hometown, each stroke survivor is completely different. But each victim of stroke I include here chose to stay standing, to work through their struggles, and to become a survivor.

To my fellow survivors, I commend you, I thank you, and I wish for all of your adventures and dreams to come true as you continue to fight the fight. Remember to keep looking for the positive in life and never give up.

 In memory of friends who are no longer with us . . .

Richard Alexander

Life before stroke: Defense attorney and world traveler.

The day it happened: He went into the restroom and noticed his face was drooping. He walked into the kitchen and fell on his back and couldn't talk.

Where we met: Austin Speech Labs.

Recovery journey: Speech, physical, and occupational therapy.

Life after stroke: He is a family man, foodie, and amateur chef, and says cooking with one hand takes longer, but he's learned how to make it fun.

Dick McCaroll

Life before stroke: Defense attorney.

The day it happened: After getting dressed for work, he sat down to eat a grapefruit. His wife asked what he was eating and he said, "Graytoo." She knew at that moment something was wrong and they went to the hospital.

Where we met: Austin Speech Labs.

Recovery journey: Speech, physical, and occupational therapy. He struggled with aphasia.

Life after stroke: Philanthropic and generous, he donated a trike to the Laredo Stroke Support Group.

Pat Crow

Life before stroke: Political consultant.

The day it happened: She had previously suffered two heart attacks. She went in for tri-pass on her heart and didn't know she had a stroke until a week later.

Where we met: Austin Speech Labs.

Recovery journey: Stroke affected the top right/front of her brain. As she put it, "Every secret I had was straight out." On top of having no filter, when she worked on speech therapy, she would kick Shilpa in the shins, but she got better with time and made an awesome comeback.

Life after stroke: Even though Pat wished she still had her old "bounce," she referred to herself as a tough old bird and I'll never forget her colorful personality.

Angie Malone

Life before stroke: National financial partner.

 The day it happened: She suffered from strong headaches at work, and finally needed to take some time off to rest.

Where I met her: Austin Speech Labs.

Recovery journey: Austin Speech Labs helped her feel confident again.

Life after stroke: As a busy mom, she had some social anxiety about getting out there again, but speech therapy helped.

Angie's message to other survivors: "Never give up! Speech and physical challenges are still a challenge for me. Just keep fighting the fight."

David Little

Life before stroke: Lawyer, marine corps.

The day it happened: He was driving his daughter to dance lessons, and had to pull over into the church parking lot.

Where we met: Austin Speech Labs.

Recovery journey: Speech therapy, chiropractic treatments, and exercise.

Life after stroke: He is the chairman of the Deacon at his church.

David's message to other survivors: "There is hope after stroke; there is life after stroke. Trust in your faith and the people around you."

Bert Bierman

Life before stroke: Assistant manager at Hill Country Telephone Cooperative.

The day it happened: It was 5:30 a.m. and he was shaving in the restroom.

Where we met: Austin Speech Labs.

Recovery journey: His entire family came  together to be his support system until he was able to take care of himself again. His dog was his guardian and stayed by his side to keep him company.

Life after stroke: He enjoys working on his garden, and kayaking. He is an avid volunteer in the stroke communities of San Antonio and Austin and wants to help other survivors in their journey.

Tom Hilgendorf

Life before stroke: Teacher.

The day it happened: He fell outside while everyone at school was attending chapel.

Where we met: Austin Speech Labs.

Recovery journey: He battled MS and stroke through speech therapy.

Life after stroke: He likes spending time with his two children, his guitar, and woodwork.

Tom's message to other survivors: "Keep going; eventually it will work out. No matter how hard it gets, just keep going."

Lacy Coleman

Life before stroke: College student, dancer.

The day it happened: At just twenty-five years old, she had congestive heart failure. The day they discharged her, as she was about to leave the hospital, she fell asleep.

Where we met: Austin Speech Labs.

Recovery journey: She worked to overcome depression; ASL gave her hope.

Life after stroke: She graduated college.

Lacey's message to other stroke survivors:

"I'm pretty lucky that I was in the right place at the right time. I was as young as I was, so that I can build up more and get better and better every day."

PJ Garza

Life before stroke: Musician, semi-pro guitarist, auto-tech student.

The day it happened: He was just twenty-four years old. All throughout high school, he

PJ, far right, with Casey, me, and Lacey at ASL Fundraiser

played sports, but because of a heart condition, he needed a pacemaker. On one of the most important games, he had to sit it out because something felt wrong. Later they realized he had a stroke. He eventually had a second stroke, six years later.

Where we met: Austin Speech Labs.

Recovery journey: Speech therapy.

Life after stroke: He likes biking and running.

PJ's words of wisdom: "Every day we are alive is beautiful. Family and friends are the biggest things."

Colin Ainsworth

Life before stroke: A cook, a college student, and a semi-pro guitarist.

The day it happened: Colin had been in a car accident less than a year before.

Colin, far right, with his family

They're still not sure if his injuries led to a stroke.

Where we met: Austin Speech Labs.

Recovery journey: Aside from speech therapy, music was an outlet for him.

Life after stroke: He also enjoys spending time in nature in his family's cabin. He attributes his energy reboot to moving from a big city (Houston) to a small town (Leakey).

Colin's words of wisdom: "Lean to the wind. Life isn't all you see."

Delvin Crenshaw

Life before stroke: Screenwriter, DJ.

The day it happened: He was with his mom and sister in the kitchen, when all of a sudden he couldn't speak.

Where we met: Austin Speech Labs.

Recovery journey: Motor skills, language and speech, and physical therapy.

Delvin, at the University of St. Augustine

Life after stroke: He is able to have some conversation, although not 100 percent yet. His ultimate goal is to be able to recover his favorite skills like DJ'ing, screenwriting . . . The sky is the limit!

Carmen Erazo

Life before stroke: Retired teacher for LISD.

The day it happened: She was taking an exercise class, and luckily there was a nurse in the class who recognized what was happening. After going to the local hospital in an ambulance, she was flown to San Antonio in a helicopter.

Where we met: Laredo Stroke Support Group.

Recovery journey: She was in a coma for several weeks. Once she came out of it, she was able to attend various therapies. Mostly, she struggled with balance issues, but was able to use a cane successfully.

Carmen, in the neon yellow at the LSSG exercise class

Life after stroke: She has lost some of her independence since she can no longer cook, drive, or exercise too rigorously. Her husband has been her support system, and she has a strong faith.

Carmen says, "God is great, and life is good!"

Peggy Newman

Life before stroke: Successful businesswoman and philanthropist.
The day it happened: It was the middle of the night.

Where we met: My friend David heard we were starting LSSG and offered to support the group since his mom was a survivor. She began to attend our meetings and the speech therapy we offered.

Recovery journey: With five grown children of her own, she wanted to recover to take care of husband who had Alzheimer's, and to continue to be the matron and nurturer of the family. It was important to her.

Life after stroke: Even though she remains an active patron in our community, she has passed the business baton to her children.

Anna Linda Davila
Life before stroke: US Courts Supervisory Clerk, case manager, and courtroom deputy.

The day it happened: One Sunday, after church, she started slurring her speech. How we met: She is the sister of my good buddy, Manuel. She started attending LSSG meetings and activities a few years ago.

Life after stroke: Her father and her husband had a stroke, too, so it became something for the whole family to learn to live with.

Hector Huerta

Life before stroke: Nashville Oil Well, multiple careers over the course of his life, very hard-working.

The day it happened: He was at work.

Where we met: LSSG.

Recovery journey: Post therapy, he is working on his leg and arm strength on his own. Some days are an emotional struggle, so it helps to have friends in LSSG. He loves biking with the LSSG Riders on Saturday mornings.

Life after stroke: He tries to be positive for others in the group.

Dan Ridge

Life before stroke: Recruiter.

The day it happened: He was in San Antonio, Texas, at the airport after a trip to Monterrey, Mexico.

Where we met: LSSG.

Recovery journey: The stroke happened down the middle (that means no aphasia or paralysis, but vision issues). He gets tired more often, but continues to stay hopeful about his future and the things that he can still do.

 Life after stroke: He is one of my favorite jokesters. He says since his stroke he has very vivid dreams, and compares them to what movie directors must see to inspire their craft. I'll keep you updated on his next movie coming out. In the meantime, he reminisces about the things he used to take for granted.

He loves cooking, playing musical instruments, and spending time with his family.

Jesse Martinez

Life before stroke: Security guard, salesman for welding store.

The day it happened: He was getting dressed for work, and his eyes started to burn. He thought he got soap in his eyes. It continued as he was driving to work, and finally he realized he needed to pull over. A bystander offered help, and they managed to call his family and 911 as he had the stroke.

Where we met: LSSG.

Recovery journey: He started with sign language (used to teach it), and his daughter started learning it to communicate with him early after the stroke.

Life after stroke: He struggles with endurance, and it's important to him. He's hard-working and wants to help his family. He was used to being the

Mr. Fix-it in their family and wants to teach his kids how.

Isabel Mendez

Life before stroke: Laredo Animal Protective Society Director, also helped her husband

with other businesses they owned.

The day it happened: It was during her seventy-fifth birthday celebration.

Where we met: LSSG.

Recovery journey: She remains active in the LSSG activities.

Her words of advice are, "Choose to stay positive; make small efforts each day."

Alex Ramos

Life before stroke: U.S. Marshall Service.

The day it happened: He collapsed in the restroom at 5:30 a.m.

Where we met: We used to coach our sons' sports teams together.

Recovery journey: Cycling and workouts helped him bounce back after therapy.

Life after stroke: He has since retired, and has an appreciation for the art of coffee-making.

Delia Mireles

Life before stroke: Teacher.

The day it happened: She had been running errands all day. She got home and had a headache, so she decided to lie down to see if it would go away. When she tried to get up, she slipped and fell as the stroke happened while she was in bed.

Where we met: LSSG.
Recovery journey: Physical, occupational, speech therapy with ASL, Art Heals program at LSSG.

Life after stroke: She learned to adapt to the new normal in her life, which took a while for others in her life to adapt to. She still ran it;

she called the shots and made sure things were done her way. "I'm the mother . . . aqui la que manda soy yo."

Fidel Cantu

Life before stroke: Educational diagnostician.

The day it happened: He had a heart attack, then a stroke, and was in a coma.

Where we met: LSSG.

Recovery journey: Depressed, doctors said he wouldn't walk again.

Life after stroke: Now he's walking, trying to stay active, and loves art therapy.

Delia Trujillo

Life before stroke: Math teacher, wellness and yoga and meditation coach.

The day it happened: She collapsed while making lunch for her son on a Sunday afternoon.

172

Where we met: LSSG.

Life after stroke: She enjoys sharing wellness with others, and writing about wellness for the local paper.

John Kilburn

Life before stroke: Professor, father, husband.

The day it happened: He had a warm rush down his back and headaches the day after being intimate with his wife, and then he started vomiting.

Where we met: Laredo Rotary Club

Recovery journey: In therapy, he let his rage fuel his performance. He pushed harder than he was supposed to and always did more than was asked, because he was going to get back and be better at things. The most important lesson he learned was to not go back and forth; make a decision and commit.

John with Deedee & I

Life after stroke: He's happier now, and understands that the recipe for happiness is simple. "Get someone to just hold your hand, be loved, relax."

David Newman

Life before stroke: David and his family owned multiple successful local businesses that he dedicated his time and energy to. He was hard-working and philanthropic in his efforts. He was an advocate for stroke awareness since stroke ran in his family and his mother is a stroke survivor. Additionally, his most important contribution to our organization was  the work he did to raise awareness for the laws surrounding caps on insurance. He worked as an intermediary for our organization and congressmen who could help us make important changes.

Where we met: We were friends since high school.

The day it happened: He was flying to see a Dallas Cowboys football game when he had a stroke in the air. He was in a coma for about two weeks. Sadly, we lost him to stroke.

Life after stroke: His legacy lives on through the work his family continues to do with the Laredo Stroke Support Group. His wife, Lulu, has now taken his place on the board of LSSG.

Ruby Olivarez

Life before stroke: Child-care licensing inspector for Texas.

The day it happened: She woke up and realized she was walking differently. Her back was hunched, and her left hand and left leg were dragging. Then  she noticed her speech was slurred. She couldn't concentrate, and there was a lot of noise.

Where we met: LSSG.

Recovery journey: She and her husband started walking together. He encouraged her more and more. She is active in Art Heals, tennis, and other LSSG activities.

Life after stroke: Ruby says, "Despite what has happened, celebrate any progress, even if it seems like they are baby steps. They are steps in the right direction."

She says joining a support group is key. To have the support of people who have gone through a similar situation helps you notice progress in each other, and gives you hope for a better tomorrow.

Johnny "Ringo" Castaneda

Life before stroke: Owned a BBQ restaurant, was very active with his family, and used to travel a lot.

The day it happened: He was shaving his head in the restroom and dropped the razor. When he picked it up, he proceeded to continue shaving and dropped the razor again. Since he had slept very little that night, he thought he must just be tired. He continued to go in to the office, and when he arrived, he tried to talk to a customer who happened to be a nurse, but his words came out as gibberish. The nurse identified that he must have had a stroke, and sent him to the hospital.

Where we met: At his restaurant.

Life after stroke: Both his friends and family have been very supportive. He's not as active as he would like to be, and does miss family trips, but he feels blessed to still be around.

Johnny says, "Listen and pay attention to your body. It will give you hints as to what is going on; you just have to pay attention. It's like the dashboard of your car. It will tell you when you need to get checked, but it's up to you to go and get it serviced before it breaks down. Do it for your loved ones."

Tony Gonzalez

Life before stroke: Retired contractor and mine worker, father to four children and grandfather to seven grandsons, tournament fisherman.

The day it happened: Tony went outside to get the newspaper, and felt dizzy. When he got back inside, he proceeded to tell his wife about feeling dizzy, but he couldn't get the words out. She realized something was wrong and called 911. He was flown from the Laredo hospital to San Antonio.

Where we met: LSSG.

Recovery journey: Speech and physical therapy at Laredo Specialty Hospital, exercise, Art Heals, tennis and other programs with LSSG, speech therapy with ASL.

Life after stroke: He is celebrating forty-seven years of marriage to his wife, Irma, and they are enjoying their grandchildren together.

Daniel Jing Gu

Life before stroke: CIO for a major bank.

The day it happened: He felt a sharp, burning pain.

Where we met: After his stroke, Daniel was in the process of forming a network for Strokefocus, and reached out to Laredo Stroke Support Group and I about collaborating. Our friendship grew from there. I enjoyed visiting with him during my trips to the Amen Clinic, since he lives in California.

Life after stroke: He may no longer be a bank executive, but he relies on the skills he has acquired to collaborate with other like-minded individuals across the globe to develop Strokefocus' network. The goal is that, one day, that network for survivors, caregivers, and medical professionals will bond together and find a cure quicker and with more funding.

Keith Taylor

Life before stroke: He was a partner in a good-sized manufacturing company and thought he had his life all planned out. He was very passionate about creating the foundation for a great retirement, which was about ten years out. Life was great—lots of family and  friends, worked hard, and played hard. Loved life.

The day it happened: He was getting ready for a business trip and was feeling off a bit. He got a call from his nephew. "What's wrong, Uncle Keith?" He asked him to stay put until he got back to him. His wife got home from work and took him to the hospital.

Recovery journey: Like everyone, his journey back has been both positive and negative at times. At first, he wondered if he had any value. He thought about suicide at one point. He had plenty of life insurance, etc., and contemplated his family being better off without him. He couldn't find anyone to help him with the depression, anxiety, and fears. Then, it hit him! "I can't be the only one going through these thoughts." He changed his mind to "How can I help others who are going through a similar experience" and began to develop tools, training, etc. for that reason. BASE is a product of that mind shift.

Life after stroke: He is very thankful to be where he is today. He gets to help others, which he is passionate about, and believes he is helping make a difference for many. He loves spending time with family and friends, and has made many new friends throughout the stroke community.

Words of Wisdom: "Stroke Survivors can re-ignite their desires in order to live a full and productive life after stroke. Does it take hard work? Yes, you are worth it!" **Believe** in yourself. **Attitude** is everything. Grow your **strengths**. Build your **energy** for a brighter future! **Develop your BASE!**

Mark Sullivan

Life before stroke: Monday to Friday, he was in a stressful job that paid very well but the cost of living in a big city "captured him in a circle of stress". Mark spent twelve hours a day sitting at his desk. Mark enjoyed ocean swimming, running, and exercise.

The day it happened: He was fixing his bike.

Where we met: On Facebook, while looking for other survivors his age who enjoyed running, cycling, and swimming. He lives in Australia & I live in Texas, but through our stroke experience we were able to connect.

Recovery journey: He viewed it as a project, and tried everything. He finds communication frustrating, but is doing all he can to help his brain heal.

Life after stroke: He stays active with exercise.

Frank Plemons

Life before stroke: Working for Dell Computer Technology Company Headquarters, very active bike riding, playing team sports, married with a son.

The day it happened: A routine thirty-two-mile loop bike ride he had done at least thirty times before on the north shore of Lake Travis turned into a freak accident when gravity pulled him into the lane of oncoming traffic. As he veered to avoid collision, he went straight into a rock wall.

Where we met: Three-way phone call with Daniel Jing Gu.

 Recovery journey: From intensive care to Saint David's Rehab Hospital, he gradually started to get the use of left arm and leg back. His prognosis was hemiplegia, and his left side was paralyzed. While confined to his hospital bed, he researched stem cell treatments and found a clinic in Tijuana called Novastem. This clinic was made popular because a hockey legend received treatment there after his stroke and was able to walk and talk almost

immediately after. Frank was intrigued, and received his first treatments two years after his stroke. He saw improvement in mental focus, arm and leg mobility, and speech three to four months after.

Life after stroke: He was out of work for about a year, and finally was able to return in a part-time capacity since his mental and physical stamina are still not where they were before. He and his wife rearranged the dynamic of their home life where she became the primary financial source for the family.

Words of advice: "Stroke survivors, do the research. Find your fit. The most important thing to look for in your health care and therapists is that they understand the brain-body connection."

Suggested Reading Lists

Books written by other stroke survivors:
1. *The Successful Stroke Survivor* by Tom Balchin
2. *My Stroke of Insight* by Jill Bolte Taylor, PhD
3. *Healing Into Possibility* by Alison Bonds Shapiro
4. *Never Give Up* by Teddy Bruschi
5. *After The Stroke* by Mark McEwen
6. *My Stroke Of Luck* by Kirk Douglas
7. *Stroke Rebel* by Linda Radestad

Some of my other favorites:
1. *Stronger after Stroke* by Peter G. Lavine
2. *Making a Good Brain Great* by Daniel G. Amen, MD
3. *A Singular View* by Frank B. Brady
4. *The Brain that Changes Itself* by Norman Doidge, MD
5. *Power Foods for the Brain* by Neal D. Barnard, MD
6. *The Blue Zone Solution* by Dan Buettner

Acknowledgements and Thanks

My siblings & my mother: Eddie Hrncir, Mary Ellen Madalinski, Nancy Johnson, and Kathleen Hrncir for taking care of your little brother and never leaving our side at the hospital. When Deedee had questions, you knew who to ask and how to get things taken care of. When I had staples to remove, Nurse Nancy came to the rescue and when we needed reminders to pray hard, Mary Ellen was there to help us keep the faith. Mom, your thoughts and prayers extended through the family and beyond. Eddie, thanks for your magic tricks and bringing your dog to break up the monotony and keep us all in good spirits.

My brother and sister in law: William "Bill" and Helen Trevino for their constant love and always inviting us to dinners on the ranch or for a walk to the lake, to remember to appreciate the presence of God in our lives and the years we have left. Bill, your music got us through so many tough times, and your Stopwatch Guy lyrics are hanging in my office as a daily reminder that there are angels among us.

185

My brother and sister in law: Stella and Hunter Burkhalter who never even flinched when their home became ours as Deedee

awaited my discharge from Texas Neuro Rebab in Austin right after the stroke. From home cooked meals, to prayers, to being a shoulder for my wife to cry on when things looked so bleak- you guys were her rock.

My brother and sister in law: Lydia and George Juarez for being the best neighbors and always offering advice- whether on important things in life (such as legal advice

and counsel) or on little day to day matters. You never run out of willingness to help, and are always there to lend a hand. Having you as board members for LSSG only meant that we could further count on your guidance and support for stroke survivors in our community. Lydi, your savory food healed us from the inside, and all of those meals as we got back on our feet meant the world to us. Thank you, also, for your meaningful edits to my rough draft.

Robert "Beto" Gutierrez, Brandy & Jeff Czar, for sponsoring my trip to London, and for supporting LSSG in numerous ways, including always buying a table for our Hope Rocks Gala.

Dara Parker & Sam Parker for your contributions and support over the years in the form of auction items, purchasing T-shirts and books, and always helping to spread the word. Reading through my rough draft, line by line, was a labor of love.

Fellow Stroke Buds, Dan Ridge & John Kilburn, for the lunch dates and your help editing my rough draft.

Hugo Chaparro & Walter Kramer, my buddies, fellow entrepreneurs, and vintage teammates, for being the sounding board for all of my speeches.

The Paul Young Family for supporting the Laredo Stroke Support Group and all of our endeavors since day one. Your generosity has helped keep us afloat and allowed us to make a difference in the lives of other survivors.

The Newman Family for your time, talent, and treasure that you've shared with our group. From your monetary contributions at every fundraiser, to your volunteered time as board members and LSSG Rider chaperones. Our group is blessed to have you in our corner.

LSSG Rider volunteers: Javier De Anda, Polo Luera, Rick Alexander, Jessie Jacaman, Jesus Torres, Melissa Guerra, Gloria "Glo" Perez, Annabel Zavala for riding alongside us and keeping us safe.

My athletic coaches: Coach Loomis, Ford, Vasquez, Allsup, and Segler for shaping me into the man I am today. Your life lessons and guidance taught me the tenacity I needed to survive this.

The Guadalupe & Lilia Martinez Foundation for your monetary contributions to Laredo Stroke Support Group. As vital as speech therapy was in my recovery, you helped us make dreams come true for other survivors.

 **My media men: Sammy "The House" & Luis Tienda Jr.** for helping us spread our mission thru PSA's, podcasts, radio

shows, and more. (George "Gar" Garza GAR Outdoors & Rey Fuentes: Matt Maldonado)

Bill Green from The Laredo Morning Times, Salo Otero and Cuate Santos (who have both now retired), for your recognition as Laredoans of the Year (which helped shed light on the needs of stroke survivors and caregivers in Laredo) and for your assistance finding articles, stats, and more to write this book.

Henry Mejia at Blue Top Printing, for helping with all of our printing needs for LSSG.

The Summers Family for your support over the years.

The youth of our community, like Daniel Serna and Paola Huerta, who are making the choice to study as therapists, doctors, nurses, etc. and return to Laredo where the stroke community needs you. Daniel, you are inspiring others through your work at Doctor's Hospital. Paola, we are proud of your accomplishments so far and we wish you the best as you pursue your Master's Degree.

Monsie Bedolla, Eli Ceja, Roger & Beth Reuweler for your dedication to the Laredo Stroke Support Group over the years. Your patience, your maturity level, and your humility have surpassed our expectations. The way you guide the stroke survivors and caregivers

means the world to us. Beth, helping me organize my thoughts and setting a framework was a crucial part of making this book happen. Your patience is much appreciated.

The mind body instructors, coaches, and trainers and massage therapists from the Laredo community like Sylvia Villarreal and Sam Lozano, whose passion for healing shines through. Our chair yoga instructors:

Diana Lowry, Irazema Espinoza, Pauline Martinez, Susana Salido, Alli Flores and the CY Ryde Coaches: Selina Chavez, Mel Ruiz, Alejandra Arguindegui, Priscilla Beckelheimer, who made working out fun and encourage us to push ourselves.

My business partners: Fred Mueller (Laredo Discount Metals) & Lalo Gou (G & H Logistics), for having the courage to trust in our relationship and know that even when I was down and out, I'd eventually get back on my feet. Neither of you asked if it would take one year, or ten, you just stood by me.

Fred saves the day! When he came to visit me at TNR, he saved a woman from a drowning vehicle.a

The hard workers at: LMS International: **Joe Guevara & Juan Cantu**, Laredo Discount Metals: **Juan Cisneros & Nancy Martinez**, and G&H Logistics: **Francisco "Paco" Cepeda & Celinda Caballero**…and all of my loyal employees. You have earned your stripes. Thank you for your patience and for sticking with us through the good times and the hard times.

My lawyer, running buddy, and friend Roby Freeman for your legal expertise and patience, and **Mary Freeman** his wife, for

being an active member of LSSG Board of Directors. Mary, your boots on the ground attitude and hard work (and delicious cookies) have gotten our group far over the years.

Hilda Mercado for her work as a board member of the Laredo Stroke Support Group, and her willingness to always offer guidance and leadership for our caregiver group.

The strong women of the LSSG caregivers and founding members group: Irma Gonzalez, Diane Davis, Crisanta Macias, Irma Martinez, Gloria Perez, Lorraine Flores, Becky Martinez, Teresa Salinas, Margie Arce, Connie Guerra, and Adela Siller.

Sonia & Guillermo "Memo" Benavides, for your support of LSSG over the years.

Patty & Moy Goldberg from Casa Raul Downtown, for your auction items and continued support of LSSG's fundraising events.
Guillermo "Memo" & Carlos "Kiko" Trevino from Southern Distributing for always being

a contributor to our Hope Rocks Gala, and other fundraisers, which allow us to serve the Laredo community.

Vaswani Family for your support of LSSG over the years.

The U.T. Health Science Center San Antonio in Laredo and Dr. Gladys Keene for providing a location for our first teletherapies with Austin Speech Labs.

The many, many therapists that I've forgotten to mention but I have not forgotten your kindness…

At Laredo Medical Center: Geronimo Santos & Laura Vargas (Laura, thank you for stepping up as a LSSG board member.)

At Austin Speech Labs:
Mayra Mata, Cassandra McGrath, Chiara Phan, Bri Rocha, Bri Fairley, Mandis Broker, Adrienne Stephens, and Jo Anne Buress.

Mayra M and I practicing my speech. She made it fun and had me prepare a commercial for Musice Milk.

At Texas Neuro Rehab: Joy Strother, Jan Muller, Tamara Traber, Marci Chandeer,

Karla Toto, Ed Varnado, Peggy Pfaff and all the others.

Dr. Darryl Camp and Mary Michelle Molina …the list goes on and on. Thank you for your patience and your kindness.

Ruthe B. Cowl & Jackie Rodriguez, J. D. Wendeborn, Ariana "Ari" Mora, Clarissa Idrogo, Nancy Rodriguez-Teller, Gloria Ceniseros, Manuel "Manny" Ceniceros, Delia Vasquez, Sylvia Lucio and Chris Martinez, for working side by side with me, as a survivor, and then with Laredo Stroke Support Group in every part of our journey. From providing therapies, to trainings, to eventually where we would house our non-profit office. J.D., your contributions as a board member of LSSG are invaluable.

Miguel Conchas and Miriam Castillo, from the Laredo Chamber of Commerce, for your guidance and resources for the Laredo Stroke Support Group. Your efforts allowed us to expand our reach within the Laredo community.

The TAMIU Nursing Program, especially Dean Marivic Torregosa, and Assistant Professor of the College of Nursing, Rosie Saldivar, Carol Gunnoe, and Gabriela Medina for their continued support of LSSG, and for allowing me to speak and raise awareness about stroke recovery.

The Laredo College OTA Program and Jodie Sandel & Lorinda Harris, for their countless Saturdays spent on the bike trail with our survivors and the LSSG Riders & Walkers.

Kristen Barta, Peggy Pfaff, and their students from the **University of St. Augustine** in Austin for your hospitality and listening to my speech. My stroke buddies and I enjoyed being your guinea pigs.

Mike & Danielle Marasco & the McDonald's Restaurant Family for your continued support and sponsorship throughout the years.

Tracy & George Mapus from La Gorra Azul Ranch and DeeDee & Tommy Martin for your generosity with all of our auctions and fundraising endeavors. Thank you for being there for Deedee and I when things got tough after the stroke. You are great friends.

Luis Martinez with Med Center for being a friend, and for your continued support.

International Bank of Commerce for your beautiful venue and staff who host our Hope Rocks Gala every year, which allows us to concentrate our profits from the evening towards our mission.

Texas Community Bank, BBVA Compass, and Falcon Bank for your sponsorship of LSSG. Thank you.

Rock Fitness & Bernadette and Helio Chapuseaux, for your partnership and for providing the perfect atmosphere for me to kickstart my recovery journey. It was here that I met my lifelong trainers and buddies.

Brittingham Family for your support of LSSG over the years.

Laredo Medical Center's Marketing Director, Priscilla Salinas and KGNS's

General Manager, Luis Villarreal and Mindy Casso, Evening News Anchor and Executive Producer, for helping us set up PSA's with KGNS when LSSG was getting started. We also benefited greatly from exposure on your Morning Chat Program. Thanks, also LMC, for your sponsorship over the years.

Judy Martinez & Dan Lopez from Doctor's Hospital for your partnership & sponsorship over the years.

Larisa Higgins & Joseph Troudt from Laredo Specialty Hospital & Annette Segovia & Teodora "Dora" Martinez from Providence Hospital for your sponsorship and sponsorship over the years, but especially for allowing us to spread the word about our program by visiting new stroke survivors and their families in your hospital rooms when they need the support most. It's scary when stroke hits, and allowing us to be there at that crucial time means they have a starting point.

LaMantia Family & L&F Distributors for your support of LSSG over the years.

Stroke Survivors throughout the United States: Angelo Seva, Cheryl Beatty, Cheryle Locke, Dan Zimmerman, David Dow,

Elizabeth Apple, Eva Arteaga, Joyce Hoffman, Kelly Reid, Neal Isaac, and Robert Meredith. You have all inspired me from afar, more than you'll ever know.

Dr. Tara Tobias, D.T. from the Orlando Neuro Therapy Youtube Channel, and **Brian McCormick**, a stroke survivor, who hosts the Stroke of the Clock Youtube Channel, stroke survivor **Mark Garman** who is the founder and host of the Determined Show on www.handinhandshow.com, stroke survivor **Rene Testa Adams** with Stroke of Luck Youtube TV Show**, Bill Monroe**, a stroke survivor with StrokeCast Podcast, and **Jerry Wald**, a stroke survivor who hosts Let's Talk Stroke with Jerry on Facebook, and **Neo** from the Road to Recovery 2020 Insta Channel. You keep my Instagram and Facebook content full of enriching reminders of what it means to be a survivor.

Some of the most influential men in our Laredo community: **Mayor Pete Saenz, Judge Tano Tijerina, Councilman Mercurio Martinez, Texas Representative Richard Raymond, and U.S. Representative Henry Cuellar** for helping spread the word about stroke awareness in our community.

To all the anonymous donors of LSSG (you know who you are): we appreciate your financial support and your friendship.

Aphasia Recovery Connection, American Stroke Association, National Stroke Association, National Aphasia Association for being reliable resources for our stroke community when we need it most.

George "Gar" Garza & Rey Fuentes with Gar Outdoors for organizing an outdoor adventure for our Stroke Survivors and documenting the fun for us to share on KGNS.

Andy Segovia for your kindness and dynamic photos in the exercise chapter of this book and on my social media.

Nic Flores for my book cover photo and your action shots used in the exercise chapter of this book and on my social media.

Matt Maldonado from Matt Ma Videos for documenting our Hope Rocks Galas and activities in such a beautiful way.

"Look at how good and pleasing it is when families live together as one."
Psalm 133:1
When the stroke happened, it happened to the whole family. I am grateful that everyone stepped up in their own way and I love you for it.

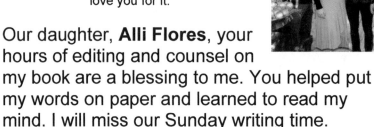

Our daughter, **Alli Flores**, your hours of editing and counsel on my book are a blessing to me. You helped put my words on paper and learned to read my mind. I will miss our Sunday writing time.

To our son-in-law, **Tony**, you dropped everything to help with anything, especially anything dealing with technology. Our daughter is blessed to have you as her "esquina".

To our son, **Billy**, you shared your college apartment with your old man for three days a week, for five years. I was your coach and for a time, you were mine. You would get after your mom for speaking for me instead of allowing me time to get my words out. I appreciate your speech knowledge and friendship.

To our daughter-in-law, **Rochelle**, thank you for sticking by Billy's side and supporting our family. Your edits on the book and your chef skills were not only needed, but appreciated.